Richard Alexander Streatfeild

Masters of Italian Music

Richard Alexander Streatfeild

Masters of Italian Music

ISBN/EAN: 9783743344686

Manufactured in Europe, USA, Canada, Australia, Japa

Cover: Foto ©Thomas Meinert / pixelio.de

Manufactured and distributed by brebook publishing software (www.brebook.com)

Richard Alexander Streatfeild

Masters of Italian Music

Masters of Italian Music

BY

R. A. STREATFEILD

WITH ILLUSTRATIONS

LONDON

OSGOOD, McILVAINE & CO.

45 ALBEMARLE STREET

1895

PREFACE

No one who ventures to write about modern Italian music can hope to avoid a certain element of monotony. At the present time, and indeed for many years past, music in Italy has meant Opera, and Opera alone. The vast majority of Italian composers devote their best energies to this peculiarly national form of art, while those who cultivate its other branches constitute a minority so insignificant as scarcely to be worthy of mention. In France and Germany Opera has divided honours with Orchestral Music and Oratorio. In Italy it has reigned supreme. In England, except at a few favoured moments, Opera has always been an exotic. At the present time, as a national form of art it is practically non-existent.

It would be tedious to discuss the various causes which have combined to make England an unoperatic country. Possibly the " honesty and energy " with

vii

PREFACE

which Matthew Arnold credits us as a race may lead us to rebel against a form of art founded altogether upon convention. Whatever the reason may be, it is certain that Opera enters far less into the musical life of England than of any Continental country. Throughout the length and breadth of France and Germany there is no town of importance which has not an Opera House, at which for several months in the year adequate if not perfect performances of popular works may be heard at a trifling cost. In England alone Opera remains the luxury of the rich. London has to be content, as a rule, with a two-months' season in the summer, while provincial towns think themselves lucky if they get a flying visit once a year from a touring company. This state of things makes it difficult to repel the charge so often brought against us of being an unmusical country. It is in vain that we cling to Handel and Mendelssohn, if we blindly ignore all the modern developments of music. How can we speak with our enemies in the gate if we know nothing of their language? Every age has had its special musical idiom. That of the present day is undoubtedly Opera. At any rate, while other forms of music appear to be gradually undergoing a process of crystallisation, the recent developments of Opera have been numerous and remarkable. Even since the death of Wagner, what new departures have we not seen? In France Massenet has taken the methods of Wagner and assimilated them in "Werther" to the characteristic structure of French opera, while Bruneau in "Le Rêve" has applied them more rigorously to a modern tale of dreamy mysticism. In Italy there has arisen a band of young men who propose to found a new school built upon a combination of German polyphony and Italian melody; while in Germany itself Humperdinck has shown in his "Hänsel und Gretel" what may be done by applying the system of Wagner to a familiar old Hausmärchen.

But it is with one only of these developments that we are concerned. During the last few years Italy, which seemed to be in serious danger of losing its right to be called the Land of Song, has been the scene of a remarkable revival of musical activity. The extraordinary development of the genius of Verdi would alone have gone far to disprove any suggestion of decadence; but among the younger generation of musicians several composers have come to the front whose works have not only achieved great and immediate success, but appear to contain the germs of what

PREFACE

*may develop in the future into something far more
solid and permanent. Lately the tendency of the
younger Italian musicians, and indeed of operatic
composers throughout Europe, has been towards melodrama of an unusually sordid and objectionable type.
It seems possible now that the fashion for work of this
kind may be on the decline. Certainly a reaction in
favour of a purer and healthier form of art could not
be headed by two works more fully instinct with the
true spirit of the beautiful than Verdi's "Falstaff"
and Humperdinck's "Hänsel und Gretel."*

*In selecting the five composers whose biographies
are included in this volume, I endeavoured to choose
the worthiest representatives of Italian music at its
best. Verdi, the prince of living musicians, naturally
heads the list. Next comes Boito, a composer whose
influence has been as extensive as his production has
been small. The rising generation is represented by
Mascagni, Puccini, and Leoncavallo—three composers
whose combined work appears to me to embrace all
that is most characteristic in the productions of the
younger musicians of Italy. The lives of these composers present special difficulties to the conscientious
biographer. The careers of the three younger men*

have been so short that they offer very little material to work with, while Verdi and Boito have already been exhaustively treated, the former in the admirable biographies of M. Arthur Pougin and Signor Barrili, the latter in the excellent article in the "Dictionary of Music and Musicians" by Signor Giannandrea Mazzucato. Brief sketches of some of the few Italian composers who have devoted themselves to instrumental music will be found in an additional chapter.

Among the composers who find no place in these pages there are several whose talents are by no means despicable. Auteri-Manzocchi and Coronaro have written operas for many years without producing anything that could possibly be considered above the second rank ; Spiro Samara is a musician of delicacy and imagination, but, though Italian by training and traditions, is by birth a Greek, and consequently does not come within the scope of this book ; Franchetti may be ranked rather as a clever amateur than as a profes-sional musician. There are many composers among the younger men, too, who have produced successful operas—Cilea, the composer of "La Tilda" ; Tasca, the composer of "A Santa Lucia" ; Cipollini, the composer of "Il Piccolo Haydn"; Mugnone, the composer of "Il Birichino"; and Giordano, the composer of " Mala Vita." In most of these works the influence of Mascagni is so very strongly marked that, in spite of their success, they can hardly be accepted as legitimate specimens of their composers' capabilities.

In conclusion, I must tender my best thanks to the firm of Ricordi, and the courteous and amiable head of their English branch, Signor Carlo Bossetti, for permission to use the interesting fragment of autobiography which is incorporated into the biography of Verdi, and for the autographs and photographs of Verdi, Boito, and Puccini with which they most kindly supplied me; to the firm of Sonzogno for valuable assistance in writing the sketches of Mascagni's and Leoncavallo's career, and for permission to publish the facsimile of a page of the score of " Cavalleria Rusticana "; to the firm of Ascherberg for so generously placing at my disposal copies of the works of Mascagni published by them; to Signor Soffredini for the opportunity, of which I gladly availed myself, of consulting the manuscript of his interesting biography of Puccini; and, lastly, to my friend Mr. R. Farquharson Sharp for his invaluable assistance in correcting the proofs.

CONTENTS

LIST OF ILLUSTRATIONS

GIUSEPPE VERDI

THERE was current some years ago among
writers on music a phrase which used to be a
perpetual source of irritation to the rising generation. It was one of those circumlocutions
dear to musical critics, and apparently indispensable to their technical vocabulary. The
phrase in question was " the last of the Titans,"
and I need hardly say that it was invariably
applied to Mendelssohn. Much as I disliked
the expression in those days, with its confident
assumption of finality and its contemptuous
ignoring of all contemporary talent, it occurs
irresistibly to my memory as I write of Giuseppe
Verdi. Only a blind admiration of the past
could refuse a place among the Titans to the

extraordinary genius who seems with each decade to have added to the fuller maturity of his genius a double portion of youthful energy and vigour, until his labours culminated (so far as the world has yet seen) in the exuberant wit and the tender wisdom of " Falstaff."

Development is the badge of the musician's trade. In music, to stand still is to recede. But though history gives us many examples of an ascent from strength to strength—Gluck, Beethoven, and Wagner, to name but three—scarcely one can parallel the story of Verdi's development.

For many years his advance was so slow as to be almost imperceptible to any but careful students of his works. From " Oberto " to " Don Carlos " the steps are small but well-defined ; with " Aida " came a sudden leap forward, and in " Otello " he threw the past finally behind him, and rose on stepping-stones of his dead self to higher things. It cannot but be a source of pride and pleasure to Englishmen that it was the genius of Shake-

speare—for, in spite of German commentators,
Shakespeare is still our peculiar and inalienable
possession—that led Verdi to heights undreamt
of before. It was not until applied to the
touchstone of our English poet that Verdi's
genius at length rang true. It is not too much
to say that he is the first and indeed the only
composer who has not only proved worthy to
collaborate with Shakespeare, but has even
thrown a new beauty upon lines familiar to
us from childhood. Verdi's career should thus
have a special interest for Englishmen, and
without undue pretension we may claim our
share in the glory of one of the greatest composers of our age.

Verdi was born on the 10th of October 1813
at Le Roncole, a poor village situated at the
foot of the Apennines, a few miles from
Busseto, a city which lies about half-way
between Parma and Piacenza. His parents,
Carlo Verdi and Luisa Utini, kept a little inn
at Le Roncole, combined with a kind of village
shop. Their house has been described as "a

3

tumble-down stone building, standing almost alone in the midst of a fertile plain sown with maize and hemp ;" but though their station was humble, it does not appear that their son ever experienced actual poverty. At the time of his birth Italy was a French province, and Busseto was therefore situated in one of the "Départements au delà des Alpes." This explains the fact of his certificate of birth being in French, and also the uncertainty which is attached to one of his names. In the certificate he is described as Joseph Fortunin François, which is Italianised in the Catalogue of the British Museum as Giuseppe Fortunino Francesco. Signor Barrili, in his Life of Verdi, suggests Fortunato or Fortunio, but the point is not of much importance, since Verdi and the world have agreed to drop all but Giuseppe.

It was eminently suitable that one whose music in after-years was to be closely associated with the cause of Italian liberty should make an early acquaintance with the terrors of war.

In 1814 Italy was the prey of the allied armies before which Eugène Beauharnais, after an intrepid resistance, had been compelled to retreat. The plains of Lombardy were overrun by the Russians and Austrians, and even a corner so remote as Le Roncole did not escape their remorseless vengeance. One morning the alarm was given that the soldiers were approaching. The terror-stricken women ran with their infants in their arms to the church, the only sanctuary which the village afforded. But even this was a poor protection from the violence of the Cossack troops, who spared neither age nor sex in their inhuman ferocity. One woman alone, Luisa Verdi, had the presence of mind to conceal herself in the narrow staircase of the Campanile, where she and her baby lay in breathless terror until the danger was past.

Verdi's first introduction to music was through the medium of a travelling fiddler, whose scraping threw the child into such ecstasies of delight that the man took upon himself to advise the elder Verdi to have his son instructed in music.

Thirty years later, when Verdi bought the estate of Sant' Agata, in the neighbourhood, he found his old friend "infirm and old" as the Last Minstrel himself, but still going his rounds with undiminished zeal. He was always welcome at Sant' Agata, and used to mumble in return for some trifling gift of money or provision, "Ah, maestro, I knew you when you were very little ; but now——"

Verdi's introduction to the organ is commemorated in another anecdote. He was then seven years old, and was assisting for the first time as acolyte in the church at Le Roncole. When the organ began to play the little boy forgot all about his duties, and stood listening in open-mouthed delight, so that the demand of the priest for water fell upon deaf ears. The story goes that, after a second or third repetition had proved equally ineffectual, the priest gave him a box on the ears which sent him rolling down the altar-steps. He was picked up insensible, but his first request when he regained consciousness was an appeal to be allowed to learn an instrument capable of producing such divine harmony. His father consented to his having lessons from the organist, whose name was Baistrocchi. He went further, and bought an old spinet for his son to amuse himself with in his leisure hours. This spinet is still in existence, and has been described with loving reverence by the late Antonio Ghislanzoni, the author of " Aida."

After three years under Baistrocchi—that is to say when he was ten years old—the little Verdi was appointed to succeed the old man on his retirement, at a salary of thirty-six francs a year, which was raised to forty francs upon the representation of the boy's father. This payment did not include the fees for marriages, baptisms, and funerals, which brought the grand total up to about a hundred francs per annum. There was a kind of tithe, too, of corn and vegetables which the organist was entitled to collect in person once a year. Verdi retained this post for seven years, in fact until he left Busseto for Milan. About the time of his appointment as organist to Le Roncole Verdi began to attend a school at Busseto. He lived there with a cobbler, a friend of his father's, who gave him board and lodging for thirty centimes a day. He appears to have been a boy of a grave and studious habit of mind. He devoted himself to work with singular application, and cared little for the games of his schoolfellows. Every Sunday and feast-day he walked over to Le Roncole before daybreak to fulfil his duties in the organ-loft. One dark Christmas morning he lost his way and fell into the canal which connects the two places, and would have perished in the icy water but for the friendly help of a passing *contadina* who fortunately happened to hear his cries for help. After two years' schooling he was taken into the warehouse of Antonio Barezzi, a merchant of Busseto, from whom his father had been in the habit of getting his stores. Verdi's entrance into Barezzi's house was undoubtedly the turning-

point in his career. Barezzi was a thorough
musician, and president of the Philharmonic
Society of Busseto, which met at his house.
The conductor of the society, Giovanni Provesi,
who was also the *maestro di cappella* of the
Cathedral, was not slow to recognise Verdi's
talent, and offered to give him lessons in counterpoint for nothing, while Barezzi kindly allowed
him to practise on his pianoforte. He
made another friend in a certain Don Pietro
Seletti, a Canon of the Cathedral, who was an
enthusiastic violinist. He taught the boy Latin,
and finding him an apt scholar, was inclined to
pooh-pooh his passion for music. "What good
will it do you?" he asked. "You are getting on
capitally with Latin; you must be a priest.
You will never make your living by music. Do
you imagine that you will ever be made organist
of Busseto?" But the Canon had to change
his mind after one Sunday morning in the Jesuit
College. The organist had failed to put in an
appearance, and Verdi was unanimously voted
to the vacant place, where he acquitted himself

excellently. After Mass the Canon asked him whose music he had been playing. "It was mine, sir," replied the boy ; " I followed my own inspiration." " Follow it always," rejoined Seletti, "and study music as much as you like. I will not advise you to drop it." Verdi did not need this encouragement to devote himself to his studies with renewed ardour. Provesi found him a most zealous pupil. He was himself a man of cultivated tastes, and, besides being an accomplished musician, was something of a poet as well. He had written both the words and music of several comic operas, some of which had been performed at Busseto. He was now no longer a young man, and the extraordinary progress which Verdi made under his tuition soon enabled him to make full use of his pupil's talents. Both in the Cathedral and at the practices of the Philharmonic Society, Verdi often took the place of the old *maestro*. Under the auspices of the latter, too, he made his *début* as a composer. He wrote many marches and other instrumental pieces for the band,

which he copied out himself and afterwards conducted. These compositions are still preserved
among the treasures of the Society's library.
Among them is Verdi's first symphony, written at
the age of fifteen, and performed at Easter 1828.

After three years of this life his friends
Barezzi and Provesi felt that Busseto no longer
gave proper scope to the talents of the ambitious
young musician. Provesi declared that Verdi
knew all that he could teach him, and more
besides, and they both felt that it was high
time for the lad to go to Milan, the musical
capital of Italy, to complete his studies. Fortunately, there was at Busseto a charitable institution called the Monte di Pietà e d'Abbondanza,
which had been founded in the seventeenth
century by those whose heirs had died during
a visitation of the plague. This institution,
among other charitable offices, supported a
public library, and gave annually four scholar-
ships of three hundred *lire* a year for four years to
assist young men who were going forth into the
world to study arts and sciences. The interest of

his patrons secured one of these for Verdi, but in his case the scholarship was commuted to six hundred *lire* a year for two years, for his friends had so firm a faith in his talents that they expected two years at Milan to turn him out a musician complete at every point—*totus teres atque rotundus*. But six hundred *lire* ($£24$) a year is not exactly a fortune ; so the generous Barezzi lent Verdi all that was necessary for his board and lodging, while his friend the Canon recommended him most warmly to his nephew Giuseppe Seletti, a professor at the *Ginnasio*, in whose house Verdi lived during his stay in the Lombard capital.

Verdi's first thought on arriving in Milan was to present himself at the *Conservatorio*. This institution was then under the direction of Francesco Basily, a very learned musician, and a pedant of the deepest dye. His counterpoint was irreproachable, but he seems to have had little sympathy with rising talent, and he failed to see anything in the youthful Verdi which indicated a promise of his subsequent success. At

any rate, there is no doubt that the future composer of "Otello" was summarily and finally
rejected. There has been a good deal of
discussion on the question of this rejection, and
friends of Basily have endeavoured to prove that
his decision was not due to any inability to
appreciate Verdi's talent, but to the fact that the
young man had already passed the age (twenty
years) after which pupils are not admitted to
the *Conservatorio*. On this point, however,
Verdi himself is the best authority, and he has
stated explicitly that his examination took place
in June 1832, when he had not completed his
nineteenth year. The theory put forward by
Fétis, that Basily rejected Verdi because he did
not see in his face any trace of artistic faculty, is
not a convincing tribute to the methods of
examination which then obtained at Milan.
Though the authorities of the *Conservatorio*
would have none of him, Verdi did not by any
means despair of himself. He was strongly
recommended to apply to Vincenzo Lavigna, a
theatrical composer of some success, and the

maestro al cembalo, or accompanist, at the theatre
of La Scala. In him Verdi found not only an
excellent master but a true friend. Lavigna
soon formed a high opinion of his pupil's merits,
and told Barezzi that he would one day be an
honour to his master and his country. Verdi
soon had an opportunity of taking humorous
vengeance on Basily. The old Professor
used occasionally to visit Lavigna, and once,
when Verdi happened to be in the room, he
began to lament the decadence of the rising
generation. "Why," said he, "the other day
there were eight-and-twenty candidates for the
post of organist to the church of S. Giovanni
di Monza, and not one of them could write a
decent fugue on the subject I gave them." "Ah,"
said Lavigna, "I have a pupil here whom I
would back against any of your eight-and-twenty.
Do you remember your subject? Let us see
what he will make of it." Basily wrote down
his subject, and Verdi sat down quietly with it in
a corner of the room. Before long he came up
with the exercise in his hand. Basily took it,

and after reading it carefully had to admit that it was excellent; but whether he recognised Lavigna's promising pupil as the rejected candidate of the *Conservatorio*, history does not relate. In 1833 the death of Provesi recalled Verdi to Busseto. He had not completed his two years at Milan, but he knew that Barezzi and his other friends wished to see him installed as organist in their own Cathedral and had indeed contributed to the expenses of his musical education principally with that object in view. So he did not hesitate, though it must have been a severe wrench to give up his studies with Lavigna and his prospects at Milan, and bury himself in the obscurity of a provincial organ-loft.

But even at Busseto it was not at all plain sailing. Provesi had never been a *persona grata* to the clerical party. He was something of a humourist, and the Cathedral authorities had occasionally been the butts of his satire. Verdi was known to have been his pupil, and, besides, during his stay in Milan had given up all his

time to secular music. So, in spite of his friendship with Seletti, he was passed over, and the
post of organist was given to a nonentity named
Ferrari, whose training had been strictly clerical.
Barezzi and the Philharmonic Society were
furious at the rejection of their *protégé*. They
had been accustomed to assist every Sunday at
the services of the Cathedral, but now they
rushed off to the Duomo, turned everything
topsy-turvy, carried off all their music, and vowed
they would never enter the building again.
This proceeding did not help Verdi much ; so
the municipality, which had hitherto paid the
Cathedral organist three hundred *lire* a year to
teach music to those who aspired to become
members of the Philharmonic, arranged to
transfer this to Verdi, whom they appointed
director of the Society. Then began an inter-
necine war between the two parties. It was a
case of Gluckists and Piccinists over again.
The town was divided into Verdiani and
Ferrariani. The quarrels between the two were
frequent, and the usually quiet streets of Busseto

were the field of many an encounter between the adherents of the rival factions. When the Cathedral chapter increased the salary of its organist, the municipality, with the assistance of the Monte di Pietà, did the same for Verdi, and went one better by christening him " Maestro di Musica del Comune e del Monte di Pietà di Busseto," which is pretty good for twenty pounds or so a year. Though excluded from the Cathedral, Verdi found a field for his talents in the chapel of the Madonnina Rossa, which belonged to a Franciscan oratory, and in the fine church of San Bartolomeo, where the Philharmonic orchestra was warmly welcomed. The service here became so famous that the Cathedral was quite deserted, and Verdi's triumph was complete. At this time he wrote a great number of masses, vespers, and motets, which were performed under his direction at one or other of these churches, while he enriched the repertory of the orchestra with endless overtures and marches, which were played on Sundays in the Piazza to the delight of the holiday-makers.

During his stay at Busseto, Verdi lived in the house of his friend Barezzi, who had been one of his most ardent supporters in all his difficulties. In 1835, at the age of twenty-three, he married Barezzi's eldest daughter Margherita, by whom he had two children. When his three years' engagement with the municipality of Busseto had expired, Verdi returned to Milan, taking with him his wife and children. He had many friends at Busseto, but his genius must have been stifled by the atmosphere of a narrow provincial town, with all its petty squabbles and scandals, and he probably felt that the more spacious life of Milan was necessary to his artistic development.

The tale of Verdi's *début* at the theatre is best told by himself. His account is already well known, but I have ventured to translate it once more, not merely because of the intrinsic interest of the events which it describes, but because of the light which it throws upon the character of the man himself:

" In 1833 or '34 there was a Choral Society in

Milan, which contained some excellent vocal material. It was conducted by a man named Masini, who, if not a very scientific musician, had at any rate any amount of patience and perseverance, very necessary qualities for the conductor of a choir of *dilettanti*. They were practising Haydn's 'Creation' and my master Lavigna asked me if I should not like to attend the rehearsals, as a part of my musical education. I accepted his proposal with alacrity.

"No one noticed the insignificant young man who sat modestly in a corner. The rehearsals were generally directed by one of three musicians, Perelli, Bonoldi, and Almasio, but one fine day, for some mysterious reason, not one of our accompanists turned up. The gentlemen and ladies of the choir showed signs of impatience, and Masini, who did not feel equal to sitting down at the piano and playing from the score, turned in despair to me and begged me for once to act as accompanist. Perhaps he could hardly be expected to have much faith in the powers of a young and unknown artist, so he added, 'It

will be enough if you only play the bass.' I was
then just fresh from my studies, and certainly
saw nothing to be afraid of in an orchestral
score. So I took my post at the piano and
made ready to begin the practice. I remember
quite well even now the half-ironical smiles of
some of the singers, and after all I suppose that
my slight boyish figure and shabby clothes were
not calculated to inspire much confidence.
Well, we began the rehearsal, and as I warmed
to my work I did not stop at merely accompanying, but began to beat time with my right hand,
playing with the left alone. I made a great
success, as great as it was unexpected. When
the practice was over I was overwhelmed by
compliments and congratulations, especially
from Count Pompeo Belgiojoso and Count
Renato Borromeo. Finally, whether the three
maestri to whom I have referred were all too
busy to keep their engagements, or for some
other reason, the matter ended in the concert
being entrusted altogether to me. It came off
with so much success that it had to be repeated.

The second performance was held in the great
hall of the Casino de' Nobili, in the presence of
the Archduke and Archduchess of Raineri and
all the grandees of the city. Not long afterwards, Count Renato Borromeo commissioned
me to compose the music to a cantata for voices
and orchestra, which as far as I remember was
to be performed at the marriage of some member of his family. I may as well say that I got
nothing for all this; it was all done for honour
and glory. Masini, who seems to have believed
in me all along, now proposed that I should
write an opera for the Teatro Filodrammatico,
where he was conductor, and gave me a *libretto*,
which was afterwards touched up here and there
by Solera, and became 'Oberto di San Bonifacio.'
I hailed the offer with delight, and returned to
Busseto, where I was engaged as organist. I
stopped at Busseto about three years. When
the opera was finished, I came back to Milan,
bringing with me the score of the opera and the
vocal parts all neatly copied out by my own
hand.

"But here my difficulties began. Masini was no longer conductor at the Filodrammatico, so the chances of getting my opera performed seemed rather remote. However, I think he must have really believed in me, or perhaps he wanted in some way or other to show his gratitude, for after the 'Creation' I had helped him several times in getting up and conducting other things, the 'Cenerentola' for one, without getting a penny for it At any rate, he told me not to be discouraged, for he would do his best to get my opera performed at La Scala for the benefit of the Pio Istituto. Count Borromeo and the advocate Pasetti promised us their support, though truth compels me to say that it never amounted to more than a few words of recommendation. Masini, on the other hand, worked nobly, and he was backed up by Merighi, the violoncello professor, who had known me when he played at the Filodrammatico, and seemed to think that I had a future before me. At last everything was arranged for the spring of 1839. I was doubly fortunate in having my work produced at La Scala, and in getting such artists as Signora Strepponi,* Signor Moriani, Signor Morini and the famous Signor Ronconi to sing it.

"The music had been given to the singers, and we were just beginning the rehearsals, when Moriani fell dangerously ill. Everything was at once broken off, and all thoughts of performing my opera were put on one side. I was left stranded, and had serious thoughts of going back to Busseto, when one morning, as I was sitting at home, up came a man from La Scala and grunted out, ' Are you the *maestro* from Parma whose opera ought to have been done for the Pio Istituto ? The manager wants to see you. Come to the theatre.' ' What do you mean ? ' said I. ' It is all right,' said he. ' The manager told me to go and bring the *maestro* whose opera was to have been done. If you are the man, come along.' And I went. The manager was a man named Bartolomeo Merelli. One evening he had

* This lady afterwards became Verdi's second wife.

heard Signora Strepponi and Ronconi talking about my opera behind the scenes in the theatre. Both of them seemed to like it exceedingly, and this was the result of his eavesdropping. When I found Merelli he came at once to business. He told me that he had heard a very good account of my opera, and wished to perform it next season. If I agreed to this I should have to make some alterations in the vocal parts, as he had not now got the four artists who were to have sung it before at his disposal. It was a noble offer. Here was I, young and unknown, and by good luck had stumbled upon an *impresario* who offered to put my new opera upon the stage without demanding payment of any sort. Merelli undertook all the expense of the production, and only bargained that, in case I managed to sell the opera, he should have half of what I received, a perfectly honourable proposal considering that I was a mere beginner. As a matter of fact, I got two thousand Austrian *lire* for it, for when the opera turned

out a success I managed to sell it to the publisher Ricordi. . . . . When the season was
over Merelli made a proposal which, as times
went, was really a magnificent one. The terms
of the contract were that I should write three
operas, one every eight months, and that they
should be produced either at Milan or at
Vienna, where he was manager of a theatre.
I was to get four thousand Austrian *lire* for
each opera and half the profits upon the sale
of the scores. Of course I jumped at the
agreement, and Merelli left for Vienna after
commissioning the poet Rossi to provide me
with a *libretto*, which turned out to be ' Il
Proscritto.'   His poem was not at all to my
taste, and I had not even begun to set it to
music when Merelli returned and told me that
I must write him a comic opera at once for the
autumn season, and then I might finish ' Il
Proscritto ' at my leisure.   I did not refuse the
proposition, and Merelli gave me several old,
forgotten *libretti* by Romani to choose from.
None of them seemed very first-rate, but I

chose the one I thought the least bad, 'Il Finto Stanislao,' which we afterwards rechristened 'Un Giorno di Regno.'

"At that time I was living in very humble quarters near the Porta Ticinese with my wife and our two children. I had scarcely settled to my new opera when I was struck down by a bad attack of quinsy, which kept me in bed for weeks. When I began to get well again I remembered that the rent, which amounted to fifty *scudi*, would be falling due in three days. The sum was not a large one even for my not too well-filled purse, but my illness had prevented my attending to business, and our exchequer had got rather low. There was no time to get the money from Busseto, so I decided to apply to Merelli for the necessary amount, either as an earnest of the payment of my contract or simply as a loan. For reasons upon which it is not necessary to dwell, Merelli failed to comply with my request. There was nothing to do but let the quarter-day pass without settling up. But my wife,

seeing my disappointment, collected the few
ornaments she possessed, went out, and somehow or other contrived to raise the necessary
sum, which she brought back in triumph. I
can hardly say how deeply I was touched by
this proof of her unselfish affection, or how
fervently I vowed to pay her back to the full
directly I got the money for my opera.

" But now began terrible troubles. My little
boy fell ill at the beginning of April. The
doctors did not seem to know what was the
matter with him, and the poor darling pined
away and died in his mother's arms. But this
was not all. A few days afterwards our little
daughter fell ill in her turn, and died, and,
to crown all, at the beginning of June my
dear wife fell a victim to a violent attack of
brain fever. On the 19th of June the third
coffin was carried from my house, and I was
left alone. In little more than two months
the three persons dearest to me upon earth
had been taken from me, and in the midst of
my terrible anguish, lest I should fail at the

appointed time, I had to sit down and write a comic opera. No wonder that ' Un Giorno di Regno ' failed. The music, I admit, was bad, but the interpretation had a good deal to do with its unfavourable reception. My private sorrows, coupled with the bitterness of this disappointment, reduced me to the lowest depths of despondency, and I made up my mind never to compose again. I did all I could to make Merelli cancel our contract. He sent for me and talked to me like a wilful child, and would not hear of my being cast down by one failure. However, I was obstinate, so he gave me back my contract, and said: ' Listen, Verdi; I cannot make you write by force, but my belief in you is unshaken. If you ever decide to take up your pen again, only let me know two months before the season begins, and I promise to produce your opera.' I thanked him, but my mind was made up, and I went away. I pitched my camp in Milan near the Corsia de' Servi. I was in very low spirits, and had given up thinking about music, when one

winter's evening I met Merelli coming out of
the Galleria De Cristoforis on his way to the
theatre. It was snowing hard, and he took
me by the arm and made me go up into his
little room in La Scala. We chatted as we
walked along, and he told me that he was in
terrible difficulties about the new opera which
he was bound to produce. He had commissioned Nicolai to write it, but the composer
was not satisfied with the *libretto*. ' Fancy
that,' said Merelli ; ' a *libretto* by Solera, on the
story of Nebuchadnezzar, stupendous, magnificent, extraordinary—such effective scenes, such
beautiful verses !—but that mule of a *maestro*
will not hear of it, and declares that it is an
impossible book. I don't know how I am to
get him another all in a moment.' ' I can get
you out of the difficulty,' I replied. ' There
is " Il Proscritto." I have not written a note
of it. It is quite at your disposal.' ' Oh,
capital : this is a real stroke of luck.' By this
time we had reached the theatre. Merelli
called Bassi, who was poet, stage-manager, call-

boy, and librarian all in one, and told him to look among the archives for a copy of 'Il Proscritto.' He soon found it, but meanwhile Merelli had seized another manuscript, which he held out to me, crying, 'See, here is Solera's *libretto!* Such a lovely plot! Fancy that man refusing it! Take it away and read it.' 'What the devil am I to do with it? Reading *libretti* is not in my line.' 'Oh, it won't hurt you to look at it; read it, and let me have it back again.' I ended by taking the manuscript. It was a huge copy written in big letters, as the custom then was. I rolled it up and started home. As I went along I felt myself possessed by a kind of vague uneasiness, a sense of despondency which amounted almost to positive pain.

"I reached my lodgings and threw the roll of manuscript upon the table. As it gradually unfolded my eye somehow caught the words,

'Va, pensiero, sull' ali dorate.'

I skimmed through the lines which followed, and was much impressed by their beauty, per-

haps because they were often almost a paraphrase
of the Bible, which I have always been fond of
reading. I read one passage, then another.
Then I remembered that I had made up my
mind not to write any more, so I shut the book
and went to bed. But all the time ' Nabucco '
was running in my head. I could not sleep,
and I ended by getting up and reading the
libretto, not once or twice, but three times, from
beginning to end, so that when morning came
I think I could almost have said it by heart.
All the same, it never occurred to me to change
my mind, so I went back to the theatre and
gave Merelli the manuscript. ' Well, it is fine,
isn't it ? ' he said. ' Very fine.' ' Set it to music,
then.' ' Not I. I'll have nothing to do with it.'
' Set it to music, set it to music.' So saying, he
took the libretto and thrust it into my coat-
pocket, seized me by the shoulders, and with one
mighty shove pushed me out of the room and
locked the door behind me. What was I to do ?
I went home with ' Nabucco ' in my pocket.
Day by day the music came to me, now one

line and now another, until bit by bit the whole opera was finished. We were then in the autumn of 1841. I remembered Merelli's promise, so I told him that 'Nabucco' was written and was ready to be performed in the next Carnival season. Merelli declared that he was ready to redeem his promise, but at the same time he pointed out that it would be impossible to produce my opera during the coming season. The programme was already arranged, three new operas by well-known composers were to be given, and to give another by one whose career had scarcely begun would be a great risk for every one concerned, for myself most of all. It would be better, he said, to wait until the spring, when he would be bound by no engagement, and he promised to engage good singers. But I refused. Either in the Carnival or not at all. I had good reasons for my obstinacy, for I knew that it would be impossible to get two artists better suited for my opera than Signora Strepponi and Signor Ronconi, who I knew were engaged, and for whom I had written the music.

"From his own point of view, Merelli's conduct was quite right. It was running a great risk to produce four operas in one season. But then I had plenty of arguments on my side, too. However, in spite of arguments and promises, the prospectus of the season was published and ' Nabucco ' was not announced in it. I was young and hot-tempered. I wrote Merelli a foolish letter, in which I gave full vent to my anger and disappointment. No sooner had I sent it off than I repented of it. I thought that I had ruined my chances once and for all. Merelli sent for me, and when I came, said angrily, ' Is this the way to write to a friend ? Never mind, you are quite right, we will do " Nabucco." But you must remember that the other new operas will be very expensive, so that I cannot afford either new scenery or costumes for you. You will have to make the best of what we already have.' I agreed, of course, so long as my opera was performed. A new prospectus was published, in which I had the delight of reading the name of ' Nabucco.' . . . . At the end of

February 1842 the rehearsals began, and twelve days after the first piano rehearsal, on the 9th of March, the first performance took place. The opera was sung by Signore Strepponi and Bellinzaghi, Signori Ronconi, Miraglia and Dérivis. With this work my artistic career really began. 'Nabucco' certainly was born under a lucky star, for everything which seemed to threaten its existence turned out well in the end. My stupid letter was alone enough to make most *impresari* throw up the whole concern. Then the threadbare costumes, judiciously patched and tinkered, looked magnificent, and the old scenery, touched up by the painter Perrani, was tremendously effective. Altogether 'Nabucco' was a real triumph. . . . . But it does not do always to trust to a lucky star. I have lived to find out the truth of our proverb 'Fidarsi è bene, ma non fidarsi è meglio' ('Trust is a good dog but distrust a better.')"

The success of " Nabucco " was very great, but it was surpassed by that of Verdi's next work, " I Lombardi alla Prima Crociata." The *libretto* of this was also the work of Solera, and though extravagant and even ludicrous in parts, it contained many fine and effective situations, of which Verdi availed himself to the full. With "Ernani," which was produced at Venice in 1844, Verdi scored another great success, and placed himself indisputably at the head of living Italian composers. At this time of day no one would care to read long accounts of operas which we now look upon as hopelessly old-fashioned, but it may be worth while to glance at some of the reasons for Verdi's great and immediate triumph. Before his advent the most popular Italian composers were Bellini and Donizetti. The former had an exquisite gift of melody, but little or no dramatic power ; the latter, though by no means without passion, had allowed his originality to be stifled by mannerisms, and during the later years of his life produced opera after opera in which to our eyes there is no perceptible difference except in the names of the characters. In looking through the long list of Donizetti's operas it is difficult to find out why one succeeded and another failed. All seem to us exactly alike. The heroes and heroines, whether French, Scotch, or Italian, always sing the same kind of airs ; there is no local colour, no characterisation, nothing but an endless stream of facile melody accompanied by the inevitable "big guitar." Into this dreary waste of nothingness Verdi burst like a breath of fresh air. His early operas, "Nabucco," "Ernani" and the rest may seem vulgar to modern ears, but there is a spirit and a directness about them which even now it is impossible to ignore. From the first, too, Verdi had a distinct feeling for characterisation. The utterances of Charles V. in "Ernani" have an undeniable element of grandeur. Silva's music, too, suggests the reserve and dignity of the Hidalgo, and the final Trio in its queer way is dramatic. We may not derive much pleasure now from a performance of "Ernani," but if we had to endure a week of Donizetti we should all go into raptures over "O Sommo Carlo."

There are two points of which it is necessary not to lose sight in discussing the success of Verdi's early works. One is the position of opera in Italy and the influence which it exercises over the middle and lower classes of the population, and the second is the special condition of the Italian people at the time when these works were produced. It is difficult for us in England to realise how deeply the opera enters into the life of a town like Milan. With us it has never been more than a luxury of the moneyed classes, and for many reasons it is never likely to be anything else. To find anything like the enthusiasm which surrounds the opera in Italy we must go in England to the music hall. There, making allowance for the difference of national characteristics, we may find a counterpart to the conditions under which Italian opera sees the light. But in the forties Milan was not the peaceable town of to-day. Ever since the fall of Napoleon Lombardy had groaned under the Austrian yoke. Whether that yoke was enforced with unnecessary harshness it is not needful to inquire. It was enough for Italians that a stranger ruled in their streets. After years of patient endurance Milan was at length ripening for the outbreak which came a few years later. In spite of Austrian espionage, the city was alive with conspiracy. The flame was ready to burst forth ; a word or a touch might ignite it. On this seething mass of sedition the melodies of Verdi smote with almost superhuman effect. Here at length was the musician of the epoch, the bard of liberty. The fire and passion of his music seemed to give voice to all the aspirations of bruised and bleeding Italy. In his stirring tunes his countrymen read the message of freedom.

There was a life and a movement about Verdi's early operas which just hit the taste of that turbulent time. On ears accustomed to the insipidities of Donizetti, " Ernani " struck like a trumpet-call. The Austrian authorities were alert and industrious censors. They wasted infinite time and pains over the *libretti* of new operas. Anything and everything that could be described as seditious was rigorously cut out. Occasionally, however, their vigilance slumbered, and sometimes the audience, which was always on the watch for an opportunity, would contrive to twist a "patriotic" sentiment out of lines which the censor had passed as innocuous.

Mr. Meredith's "Vittoria" is the *locus classicus* for a *première* at La Scala during those troubled days. His famous description of the production of "Camilla" is not merely one of the most glowing pieces of word-painting in the language, but gives a singularly vivid and truthful picture of the stormy scenes which at that time attended the birth of a new opera by a popular composer.

Verdi was always in difficulties with the authorities, and few of his operas saw the light without a trimming from the judicious Austrian pruning-knife. But even in their mutilated state they spoke with no uncertain sound to the passionate patriotism of Italy. The famous chorus from "Nabucco," "O mia patria si bella e perduta" ran like wild-fire from lip to lip, and

the united voices of his countrymen proclaimed
Verdi the Tyrtæus of Italian freedom.

The success of "Ernani" set the seal upon
Verdi's popularity. He was at once besieged
with demands for far more operas than he could
hope to supply. The natural result came to pass.
For the next few years he produced nothing
which has survived to our times, nothing which
deserved to survive. He was working against
time, and all that he wrote at this period bears
the mark of haste and hurry. As his next
four operas have vanished once and for all from
the current *répertoire*, it would serve no good
purpose to describe them at length. "I Due
Foscari" (1844), founded upon Byron's tragedy ;
"Giovanna d'Arco" (1845), which owed what
success it achieved to the genius of Erminia
Frezzolini ; "Alzira" (1845), and "Attila" (1846),
may be passed over in a few words. Whatever is
good in them is merely a reproduction of the
most salient features of "Ernani" and "I Lombardi," and even in Italy they seem never to
have had any pretensions to more than ephemeral

success. The weakness of these works is indeed
not altogether Verdi's fault. The *libretti* which
he had to set to music were the most terrible
balderdash imaginable. He was haunted at this
time by two "poets," Cammarano and Piave,
who vied with each other in producing masterpieces of inane doggerel. It was through the
medium of Piave that he first made the acquaintance of Shakespeare, from whom he was afterwards to draw the inspiration for his noblest
works. Unfortunately for Verdi, in 1847 Boito,
the future author of "Otello" and "Falstaff,"
was still in the nursery, and the adaptation of
"Macbeth" fell into the hands of Piave. The
result was not inspiring, but nevertheless Verdi
wrote to this *libretto* better music than he had
yet given to the world. With a more sympathetic collaborator he might even then have
produced a masterpiece. In a country which
knew its Shakespeare, "Macbeth" would have
been foredoomed to failure, for Lady Macbeth
trolling a drinking song, and a ballet of witches,
would have been rather too much even for the

patience of an operatic audience. Italian
audiences had no scruples on these points,
but they objected as a rule to an opera
without any love-making. However, "Macbeth" undoubtedly did succeed, though it is
probable that a certain amount of the goodwill
extended to it was due to the fact that the
audience saw in the fall of the usurper a presage
of the destruction of Austrian power in Italy.
The *clou* of the piece was the duet sung by
Macduff and Malcolm under the towers of
Dunsinane, "La patria tradita piangendo c' in-
vita," which never failed to excite a frenzy of
enthusiasm. But apart from politics, there is
some really good music in "Macbeth." The
sleep-walking scene is admirable in an old-
fashioned way, and Macbeth has some fine
declamatory music quite on a par with parts of
" Rigoletto."

Altogether, there is music in "Macbeth"
which is worthy of study to those who desire to
trace the development of the composer's genius,
and I should be inclined to quote this opera as

the first in which Verdi put off the wild storm and stress of his early manner and began to think more seriously of fitting the note to the word and the word to the note. In " Macbeth," too, for the first time, he begins to feel uneasy in the fetters of the *bel canto*, and occasionally allows his characters to sing a passage which could not be instantly snapped up and labelled as a tune and despatched to the organ-grinders. When the opera was performed in Paris in 1865, a good deal of the music was re-written, and what was left was subjected to revision. The last scene in its present form dates almost entirely from this period. It is the best part of the opera, and in some ways one of the finest acts Verdi has ever written. There is some admirable choral writing in it, and the battle-scene, a vigorous *fugato* developed with spirit and ingenuity, is singularly effective.

The following letter, which dates from the beginning of 1847, throws some light upon the amount of work which Verdi had on his hands at this time. It is one of a small collection at the British Museum, none of which have hitherto been published. It was written to M. Léon Escudier, a member of the firm which published Verdi's works in France.

" Pray, forgive my slowness in answering your letter. I have been rather lazy, I know, but I have an immense amount of work on hand as well. Many thanks for the notices of ' I due Foscari ' and ' Roberto Bruce.' * I read an article in the *Débats* on the latter by Berlioz, which is interesting to any one who means to write for the ' Opéra.' I have heard from your brother as well as yourself about writing an opera for the 'Italiens,' but I am afraid that I can't manage it. I do not like making new contracts till the old are off my hands. You can't conceive how my engagements bother me. When I shall have fulfilled them all, I don't know. Before long, ' Macbeth ' will be finished. That will be one opera off my hands. I have decided on ' I Masnadieri ' for

* An opera by Rossini, which had just been produced in Paris.

44

London. I have got the *libretto*, which seems a good one. It is by one of our best writers, so at any rate the poetry is all right, and the situations are effective too. I shall see you on my way to England, but I wonder when I shall hear one of my works at the 'Opéra.' Do you know for certain whether Meyerbeer is going to London? I wish you would find out and let me know."

As Verdi's next work, " I Masnadieri," was written for the English stage, I will take this opportunity of glancing back over the reception which had been given to his earlier operas in this country. We are not, as a nation, in the habit of being quite abreast with the newest movements in the world of music, and it was not until 1845, after the production of " Ernani," when he had already been famous in Italy some time, that he was introduced to England. Before then, however, faint echoes of his fame had reached these shores. Chorley, in the *Athenæum*, had dedicated to the young composer a notice, from which I intend to make a few extracts, not on account of the criticism he devotes to those of Verdi's published works which had reached him, but because some of his remarks help one to realise the condition of opera as it was at the time, or, at any rate, as it appeared to a critic of pronouncedly conservative tendencies :

" Recent occurrences and appearances having called the attention of our English public to the modern style, or rather no-style, of Italian singing, it may be as well for the critic to see what is doing in the world of Italian vocal composition ; and, since the name of Giuseppe Verdi has begun to circulate widely as the *maestro* most likely to become popular, we will avail ourselves of such opportunities as perusal of his compositions here published affords us, to offer a word or two concerning his operas.

" But, first, we must remind the reader that the distinctive basis of Italian opera, from its outset, has been melody—melody in recitative, in air, in concerted piece, and in chorus—the dramatic expression being largely left to the singer. Even in the German musical drama, though the voice has been often assigned tasks

too ungracious to be ever well performed, under
the notion of rendering it a mere instrument in
the composer's hands, and the adaptation of
sound to sense has been more closely studied,
still melody has been indispensable to success—in the orchestra if not on the stage.
Digressing for a moment, we may add that at
certain points the fusion of the two schools has
taken place, as in Mozart's operas. But whether
German or Italian, there is no melodist who has
not had a way of his own, in part arising from
those mysterious instincts which defy analysis,
in part referable to the executive power or
prevailing fashion of the composer's age, and,
beyond these, that *je ne sais quoi* which the ear
learns to distinguish as surely as the eye decides
on the touch of the painter. Now, it appears
to be the fancy of the modern European school
to throw overboard what is essential because of
the accidental; and, since invention just now
seems to be at the lowest ebb of exhaustion,
musicians denounce the old manner of satisfying
the ear as mere excitement *ad captandum*. In

France, for instance, M. Berlioz does vigorous battle with rhythm, quoting, with admirable inconsistency, Gluck's colossal style against Auber's piquant measures ; forgetting that the structure of all Gluck's great melodic pieces is as referable to the Ciaconna, Gavotte, and Minuet taste of his epoch, as M. Auber's livelist Finale is to the Galop or the Valse which has succeeded those more solemn measures. All this while, be it noted, M. Berlioz, whenever he does employ a form in his own compositions (and without form and number, whatever be the mode of arrangement, there can be no musical composition better than the wanderings of an Eolian harp), adopts one of the most hackneyed commonplace and frivolity. Then there is Herr Wagner, the young Dresden composer, whose operas we have heard rapturously bepraised, because they contain no tunes which any one can carry away. Yet we do not hear that in declamatory propriety and dramatic fashion he has improved upon Weber, the deepest of German vocal composers, and still the most sympathetically melodious and fascinating.

"In Italy, as all the world knows, Bellini, eager to throw off the symmetrical forms of Rossini with small expense of study or labour, established a manner striking in its languid *laisser aller*. But, under pretence of dramatising the style of Italian Opera, Bellini's successors, less vigorous in invention, have outdone him in renouncing all firmness and ordinance of construction, producing, it is true, tunes in the canonical number of bars required by the poetic ear, but without the slightest novelty of combination or phrase. In short, Italian invention seems fast advancing towards a point at which, whether the idea be old or new it matters little, so that the singer has a *spianato* passage to bawl or to sigh out, either *solus* or in unison with his comrades, a semblance of intensity and contrivance being given by a use of the orchestra licentious enough to make Cimarosa and Paesiello (those colourists as tender but as consummate in their art as Watteau) turn in their graves.

"Time may reconcile us to these strange

principles : we may come to value music in
proportion as all form and feature are effaced,
and see, without a sigh, the opera reduced to
the shapeless recitative from whence it arose—
with this difference, that whereas the voice was
of old only supported by a chitarra or a
violone, it will be smothered, under the new
dispensation, by what the Germans call 'janis-
sary music.' Till, however, we reach this state
of vitiated taste, we must conceive the ancient
standards to be in the main equitable, and try
new productions thereby."

Chorley then gives a short sketch of Verdi's
career, and proceeds to the discussion of his
works.

"For new melody we have searched in vain,
nor have we even found any variety of form,
indicating an original fancy at work as charac-
teristically as in one of Pacini's, or Mercadante's, or Donizetti's better cavatinas. All
seems worn and hackneyed and unmeaning.
. . . . Signor Verdi's concerted music strikes
us as a shade worthier and more individual

than his songs. There are intentions, though the fillings-up be weak to puerility, in his duet for Ernani and Silva, and the effect of the 'Congiura' chorus is probably striking, with the mass of voices and orchestra, though the unisons be surfeiting. These, by the way, first employed by Rossini in his 'Gazza Ladra,' offer a rare expedient to the easily-contented and the ill-assured. To judge from the crudity of Signor Verdi's harmonics and progressions, he belongs to the latter class, who 'think they are thinking.' . . . . We cannot conclude these brief remarks—incomplete, for obvious reasons, as a judgment—without saying, that, flimsy as we fancy Signor Verdi's science, and devoid as he seems to be of that fresh and sweet melody which we shall never cease to relish and welcome, there is a certain aspiration in his works which deserves recognition, and may lead him to produce compositions which will command respect."

The reception of his works on this side of the Channel soon showed Verdi the difference between England and Italy. Here, of course, the special conditions which did so much to fan the flame of his success at home were entirely absent. In a country remote from the frenzy of political agitation the critics soon found out the weak points in his armour. "With every sympathy," wrote Chorley, "in favour of a new style and a new master, our first hearing of 'Nino'* has done nothing to change our judgment of the limited nature of Signor Verdi's resources. He has hitherto shown no power as a melodist. Neither in 'Ernani' nor in 'I Lombardi,' nor in the work just introduced, is there a single air of which the ear will not lose hold. The most hackneyed forms of Donizetti seem to have served as the composer's starting-point of invention. But he can be very animated in the distribution of old materials. . . . . Signor Verdi's *forte* is declamatory music of the highest passion. In this, never hesitating to

* "Nabucco" was performed under this name in England, with an altered *libretto*.

force an effect, or to drive the singers to the
'most hazardous passes :' he is justified for
some extravagance by an occasional burst of
brilliancy surpassing that of most modern
composers. . . . . But he is nothing if not
noisy, and by perpetually putting forth his
energies in one and the same direction,
tempts us, out of contradiction, to long for
the sweetest piece of sickliness which Paesiello
put forth long ere the notion of an orchestra
had reached Italy or the singer's art was
thought to mean a superhuman force of
lungs."

The extravagance of "Ernani" is certainly
undeniable, but it seems odd that Verdi should
be denied the gift of melody. However, Fétis
declared that there was not the semblance of a
tune in the overture to "Tannhäuser," so that
at any rate Verdi suffered in distinguished
company.

The attitude of the English public was very
different from that of the critics. From the
first Verdi had been a favourite in London,

53

and the production of "Ernani" placed his popularity upon a sure foundation. But crowded houses at Covent Garden and Her Majesty's could not convince the obstinate conservatism of Chorley and his friends. A letter in the *Athenæum* of January 1844, protesting against the systematic disparagement of Verdi and his works in that journal, is interesting, not only as a testimony to the popular estimate of the Italian *maestro*, but as a proof that even in the dark ages the general public occasionally issued a protest against the ignorance and incompetence of musical critics.

Verdi's popularity in London was so great that Mr. Lumley, the manager of Her Majesty's Theatre, felt justified in commissioning him to compose an opera expressly for the London stage, to be produced under his own direction. "I Masnadieri" was the result. The *libretto*, written by no less famous a man than the poet Maffei, was founded upon Schiller's "Die Räuber," and the idol of London, Jenny Lind, sang the *rôle* of the heroine. Nevertheless, the opera was coldly received, and was perhaps the least successful of all his works. Chorley pronounced it the worst opera ever produced in Her Majesty's Theatre. One of its few successful features was a violoncello solo in the overture, which was played by Signor Piatti.

The failure of "I Masnadieri" had probably something to do with Verdi's decision in a matter which might have altered the whole current of his life. Mr. Beale, who had just started the rival establishment at Covent Garden, had succeeded in seducing Sir Michael Costa from his allegiance to Mr. Lumley. The latter did all in his power to prevail upon Verdi to accept the vacant post of conductor. It is possible that he might have succeeded had not the composer's engagement with the publisher, Francesco Lucca, weighed upon his conscience. He had promised to compose two operas for him by a given time, and this, combined with the failure of "I Masnadieri," which was calculated to prejudice him against England, induced him to refuse the offer. Disappointed and humiliated, he left the shores of England, never to return except for a couple of flying visits. Since 1862, indeed, he has allowed his aversion to the sea—an aversion which he shared with Rossini—to prevent him crossing the English Channel, and not even the offer of an honorary degree at Cambridge could induce him to repeat the hazardous experiment. Verdi did not get further than Paris on his way home. At the Opera they were rehearsing a revised version of his " Lombardi," to which a new libretto had been arranged. This was successfully produced in November as " Jérusalem." After this event Verdi retired to Passy, where he took a house and devoted himself to the composition of his two new operas, " Il Corsaro " and " La Battaglia di Legnano." Neither of these works show the composer even at his second best. His English trip had not been a success, his health was affected by worry and overwork, and he was far too good a Liberal to be able to sit down peacefully to work while his country was in the throes of revolution. Probably all these reasons reacted to a certain extent on his music. "Il Corsaro," written to a *libretto* by Piave on Byron's poem, was a thorough failure, and " La Battaglia di Legnano," though its patriotic subject fitted in with the feverish excitement of 1849, and gave it an ephemeral success, never bore revival, and even in 1861, when it was given at Milan for the first time, it sounded old-fashioned. This was one of Verdi's operas to which the Austrian censors raised objections. In this case the difficulties were easily smoothed over. A mere change of name was enough. The scene was transferred to the Low Countries, Barbarossa became the Duke of Alva, and "La Battaglia di Legnano " was re-christened " L'Assedio di Harlem." By such measures as this the Government flattered itself that sedition would be averted.

After the production of "La Battaglia di Legnano" Verdi returned to Paris and hard work. But he did not stay long ; 1849 was the year of the terrible outbreak of cholera in Paris, and before that awful invader Verdi thought it wise to retire. He took with him the finished score of a new opera, "Luisa Miller," which had been commissioned by the *impresario* of the Teatro di San Carlo at Naples. When, after a weary period of quarantine, he finally arrived at his destination, it was only to find the manager bankrupt and the theatre closed. Verdi was preparing to retreat, but the Neapolitans, not wishing to lose the chance of hearing a new opera by the popular *maestro*, did all in their power to detain him, or, at any rate, to induce him to leave his MS. behind him.

Verdi was on the point of taking refuge on board an English man-of-war, when fortunately affairs at the San Carlo were once more adjusted, and " Luisa Miller " was at once put into rehearsal. It was produced with genuine success on the 8th of December, a success which must have been all the more welcome after the very doubtful reception of the composer's last three works. Many critics see in " Luisa Miller " the beginning of what they are pleased to call Verdi's " second manner." If second manner there be, I should prefer to date it myself from " Macbeth," but there is no doubt that " Luisa Miller " shows a marked advance on the style of " Ernani" and other works of that period. The libretto, founded by Cammarano on Schiller's tragedy " Kabale und Liebe," is a poor enough piece of work. It is uncommonly long-winded, and until the last act there is no situation of any real dramatic interest. But Verdi contrived for once to put his grandiose manner aside, and to treat the story with the requisite simplicity and with a refinement for which hitherto he had not been conspicuous. The opening scene is a charming idyll, and foreshadows very strikingly the exquisite flower-chorus in " Otello," while the last act throughout is most pathetically treated. A good deal of this act, especially the beautiful duet between the father and daughter, recalls a similar situation in " Rigoletto," and indeed is scarcely, if

at all, inferior to it. It is rather curious that
" Luisa Miller " should have dropped so entirely
out of the current *répertoire*, for the heroine's
music is not only melodious, but in places highly
dramatic, and at least as effective as that of " La
Traviata." The heavy father is certainly not
an amusing person, and there are two very
villainous basses who indulge in gloomy and
protracted duets, but a good deal of the opera
could not fail to delight any one who still has
ears for the beauties of " Rigoletto."

Verdi's next work, " Stiffelio," which was performed at Trieste on the 16th of November
1850, seems to have been a complete failure.
An opera with a Lutheran pastor for hero
certainly does not sound promising. The composer, however, evidently thought his music
worth preserving, for he subsequently had a
new *libretto* written to it, and with sundry other
changes the work was given as " Aroldo " at
Rimini, in 1857. Even then its bad luck clung
to it and nothing could make it a success. The
music is thoroughly in the " Rigoletto " style,

and much of it is melodious and effective, but
the libretto is hopelessly dull and exceedingly
offensive into the bargain ; so perhaps it is as
well that the opera has been consigned to
oblivion.

We have now reached a very brilliant period
in Verdi's career, a period marked by the production of " Rigoletto," " Il Trovatore," and
" La Traviata," three works, which, in spite of
all the changes of taste and fashion, have held
their own manfully against all new-comers.
There were a good many difficulties to be over-
come before " Rigoletto " could see the light.
The libretto, founded by Piave upon Victor
Hugo's play, " Le Roi s'amuse," did not at all
recommend itself to the Austrian authorities.
In justice to themselves they could not dream
of allowing King Francis I., who is the hero of
the original play, to appear on the stage of La
Fenice under such extremely equivocal circumstances. It would have been a downright insult
to the monarchical principle. Luckily one of the
Austrian police officers found a way out of the

difficulty. The *locale* of the story was changed
to Italy, the King became a Duke of Mantua,
and the title of the opera, to which objection
had also been made, it is difficult to see why,
was altered from "La Maledizione" to "Rigoletto." Thus every one's scruples were satisfied,
and Verdi, who had not as yet written a bar of
the music, retired to Busseto to compose it.
He must have received a double measure of
inspiration from his native air, for in forty
days the score was written and orchestrated.
The opera was at once put into rehearsal,
and was produced at Venice on the 11th
of March 1851 with the most unbounded
success.

Verdi was always a great favourite at Venice,
and several of his most successful operas were
written for the Fenice Theatre. Ever since the
days of Monteverde the Venetians had been
enthusiastic lovers of opera, and the Fenice
audience was one of the most sympathetic in
Italy. There is a good story, *à propos* of the
production of "Rigoletto," which illustrates the

quickness of the Venetians in musical matters.
It has often been told before, but may bear
repeating once more. When the *rôles* were
distributed, the tenor who was to play the Duke
found a blank in his part at the beginning of
the third act. He went to Verdi and asked
him what it meant. "Don't be in a hurry,"
said the *maestro*, "there is plenty of time."
Every day it was the same story; the tenor
petitioned in vain for his missing song. At
last, the day before the final rehearsal, Verdi
gave him the manuscript of the famous "La
donna è mobile," but not before he had made
him promise not to sing or whistle a note of it
to a living soul. At the rehearsal every one was
laid under a solemn oath not to divulge a note
of the music before the performance. Verdi
knew the quickness of Venetian ears. He
knew that if the melody of the song were once
heard outside the walls of the theatre, it would
be all over Venice in a few hours, and at the
performance the gilt would be off the ginger-
bread. The secret was well kept, and the

"Canzone" was the success of the evening, but on the way home every one was humming the air, and by the next day it was the common property of every *gamin* in Venice.

"Rigoletto" is in many ways a landmark in the history of Verdi's development. Apart from the passion and beauty of the music, it marks an era in the history of Italian Opera. In "Rigoletto" we find for the first time the aria displaced by the declamatory monologue.

To realise the importance of this new departure, it will be necessary to glance back at the development of Italian Opera before the days of Verdi. During the period of which Handel is the most famous representative, an opera consisted practically of a series of airs (often as many as thirty in an opera) connected by *recitativo secco;* that is to say, recitative accompanied by the harpsichord. After Handel's time *recitativo secco* was gradually displaced in serious opera by *recitativo stromentato*, recitative accompanied by the full orchestra, the invention of which is generally attributed to Scarlatti.

FACSIMILE OF AUTOGRAPH SCORE BY VERDI

"*Rigoletto*," *Act III., Quartet.*

A further development of this, and one which is of the greatest importance in the history of opera, is generally attributed to Gluck. It may conveniently be termed rhythmical declamation, and it is especially interesting as embodying the earliest attempt to use the orchestra as something more than a mere accompaniment to the voices. There is a good example of it in the last act of " Orfeo," just before the famous song " Che farò." The orchestra here has a rhythmical subject, entirely independent of the voice. In Grétry's words, the statue is in the orchestra and the pedestal on the stage. This rhythmical declamation is the foundation of all modern opera. It is the parent of Wagner's "endless melody," and in our day has completely superseded the conventional airs and duets of the earlier school. But at the period from which " Rigoletto " dates, rhythmical declamation, at any rate in Italy, had not reached a very high stage of development. It was a slave to four-bar rhythm, which was apt to engender monotony, in spite of the ingenuity which was often displayed

in developing the theme. Opera, then, during
Verdi's early period consisted of recitative,
rhythmical declamation, and, at critical points
in the drama, airs, duets, and concerted pieces.
In "Rigoletto" we find for the first time a solo
which is too fully accompanied and too rhythmical in structure to be recitative, too declamatory for an air, and entirely free from the des-
potism of four-bar rhythm. The solo in question is Rigoletto's great monologue in the second
scene of the first Act, beginning "Pari siamo,"
founded upon a famous speech in "Le Roi
S'amuse." How far Verdi had advanced since
the days of "Ernani" can be seen at a glance
by comparing his treatment of Rigoletto's
monologue with that of Charles V. in the earlier
work. What a leap from the bareness and conventionality of the one, to the varied colouring
and passionate force of the other! The position
of this scene, too, in the drama is an illustration
of the greater flexibility of Verdi's new method.
Rigoletto's monologue comes between two
scenes which are examples of rhythmical decla-

mation at its best. In both cases the scene is
constructed almost entirely upon a phrase of four
bars, and though Verdi has contrived to infuse a
high degree of feeling and intensity even into the
old-fashioned medium, we feel that when we
reach the monologue we are in a different world ;
it is like coming from chains and a dungeon
into the free light of day. But in many other
ways " Rigoletto " is an advance upon its predecessors. In his treatment of the Aria in this
opera Verdi shows a sublime indifference to
tradition—the tradition of the Cavatina and
Cabaletta, the slow movement followed by the
quick—which hitherto had been the almost in-
variable rule in Italian Opera. It is true that
in " Rigoletto " the older form still survives.
The Duke's air at the beginning of the second
Act is faithful to the old convention, but it is
followed by Rigoletto's great scene with the
courtiers, which is treated with the utmost
freedom. This again is followed by the duet
between father and daughter, in which Verdi
returns once more to the old plan. Indeed, so

far as concerns his treatment of the Aria, we must look upon "Rigoletto" as a work of transition. As a matter of fact, Verdi did not finally break with the Cavatina-Cabaletta tradition until he wrote "Aida," twenty years later, and even there the curious may find lingering traces of the old habit.

After the production of "Rigoletto" Verdi allowed himself a brief respite from his almost ceaseless labours. But even when he was busiest he found time to keep abreast of musical events at home and abroad. Here is a characteristic letter, dated September 30, 1851, to M. Marie Escudier:

"I am delighted to hear about your trip to London. I like hearing about all the sights and festivities. It seems to have been a successful season at the Opera. I hope your season in Paris will be equally good. You are rather in trouble about your singers, but at any rate you have got two new *prime donne*, which is something. I wonder if Signora Barbieri will be a success? You see I am as inquisitive as

ever, even here in my out-of-the-way corner.
If Lumley* is wise, he will bring her out
in 'Lucrezia Borgia.' How does Hiller† conduct? He has been in Italy of course, but
that must have been ten or fifteen years
ago, and I don't suppose he has seen or
heard any of our operas since then. What
can he know about conducting Italian opera?
We do things so differently from you. I
don't say which is right, but you know what
I mean. These grandees from Academies and
Conservatoires shudder at the thought of a fifth
or an octave, and as for a tune, they would
make it a penal offence to write one. Yes:
for Italian operas we want Italian conductors.
You know what a crank I am, but that is my
fixed opinion. But what does it matter? I
shall be happy enough, whatever happens at

* Mr. Lumley was at that time manager of the
Théâtre Italien in Paris.
† Ferdinand Hiller, the composer of the "Song of
Victory," who was conductor at the Théâtre Italien for
two seasons.

the Théâtre Italien. What the devil am I
doing now? I have actually written you two
pages all about music, when you know I care
not a pin's head about the whole concern.
However, it is done now, so the letter shall go
as it is."

It is a curious fact that after the composition
of "Rigoletto," instead of hastening along the
path of development on which he had started
so auspiciously, Verdi fell back once more
into his earlier manner. In every possible
way "Il Trovatore" shows a falling off from
"Rigoletto." With it we go back once more
to the Cavatina-Cabaletta period, back to
the old ranting style of "I Lombardi,"
back to the aimless and uncharacteristic
tunefulness of "Ernani." In "Rigoletto" the
melodies are simple and obvious enough to
captivate the most uncultivated ear, but they
are always more or less in keeping with the
character of the person who sings them. Even
"La donna è mobile," hackneyed as it is,
always delights us on the stage because it so

thoroughly expresses the frivolous pleasure-seeking nature of the Duke. But in "Il Trovatore" the tunes are, so to speak, slung together anyhow without any regard to situation or character.

What is the explanation of this strange falling-off? One would be tempted to suppose that "Il Trovatore" must have been written first, and for some reason kept in the composer's portfolio until after the production of "Rigoletto." But Verdi's popularity was so great that whatever he wrote was at once snapped up by the managers. Besides, if "Il Trovatore" had been written in 1851 there would probably have been some talk of performing it in place of "Rigoletto" at Venice when the *libretto* of the latter was forbidden by the Austrian censors. It happened, too, that a longer period than usual elapsed between the production of these two operas —nearly two years—so that Verdi had plenty of time, had he been so inclined, to alter or even rewrite the score of "Il Trovatore" before its production. A possible explanation of the anomaly may lie in the different standard of musical culture in Northern and Central Italy. "Rigoletto" was written for Venice and "Il Trovatore" for Rome, and the kind of music which would recommend itself to the *dilettanti* of Venetia or Lombardy might very possibly be too advanced for the less cultivated palate of the Eternal City. Even in England the standard of musical taste is often curiously different in two neighbouring towns. In Italy the distinction is as a rule far more strongly marked. Verdi's habitual shrewdness may have guided him aright in this instance, for the first performance of "Il Trovatore" was a real triumph, and this initial success probably had a good deal to do with its subsequent popularity. If this is the explanation, it is certainly more creditable to Verdi's sagacity than to his artistic conscience. But the *libretto* of "Il Trovatore" is really quite enough to explain and excuse far worse music than Verdi actually wrote for it. Although founded upon a tragedy which had been popular for years in Spain and Italy, it is a farrago of the most incomprehensible rubbish ever written. In the happy days to come, when the post of musical critic will only be attainable by competitive examination, I shall sympathise profoundly with the unlucky candidates who are called upon to write a brief sketch of the plot of " Il Trovatore." I suspect that very few even of our most experienced critics could tell us exactly who Urgel was and what happened at Pelilla.

If " Il Trovatore " errs on the side of coarseness and vulgarity, the fault was soon corrected, for in " La Traviata," which was produced a few months afterwards, a laudable striving after delicacy and refinement occasionally landed the composer in positive feebleness. Anything less worthy of the situation than " Parigi, o cara," or the baritone romance " Di Provenza il mare," could scarcely be imagined, and both are singularly remote from Verdi's usually vigorous method. But the story of " La Dame aux Caméllias " was altogether different from anything he had yet attempted. Dumas's play, morbid and sickly as much of it is, has a psychological interest which it would be vain to seek in any of the *libretti* which Verdi had previously undertaken. It was a *tour de force* for a man, who had hitherto dealt almost entirely in melodrama of the most transpontine description, to succeed so brilliantly in " drawing-room tragedy." Much of " La Traviata " is so beautiful that it seems a pity it should have degenerated into a mere *prima donna's* opera, only to be given from time to time with the " scratchest " of casts in order to allow a popular singer to show off her high notes and her diamonds. At its first performance " La Traviata " was a pronounced failure. The cast seems to have been a bad one, the consumptive heroine being represented by a lady of prodigious stoutness, and the modern dress, which then was used, probably had something to do with its want of success. But it soon won its way to popular favour, and in time became one of the most frequently performed of all Verdi's works.

74

Before the days of "Rigoletto," "Il Trovatore," and "La Traviata," Verdi had been
popular and famous, but outside the bound-
aries of Italy critics were by no means unanimous as to his genius. In England and France
particularly there were, as we have seen,
many who looked upon him as a mere devotee
of the big drum and cymbals, and, stranger
still, denied his claim to any melodic gift
whatsoever. After 1853, however, he had
the world at his feet, and one of the first
proofs that Paris, the stronghold of musical
Chauvinism, had at length hauled down her
colours, was an invitation to write an opera
for the Académie Impériale de Musique, to
be produced in 1855 during the Universal
Exhibition. Verdi accepted the proposition,
and betook himself to Paris to begin the
composition of the work. The opera in
question was "Les Vêpres Siciliennes," the
libretto being by Scribe and Duveyrier. Verdi
had finished his score by September 1854, but
the opera was not actually produced until the

75

following June, partly owing to difficulties with the band as to rehearsals—for Verdi was rather an autocrat, and the orchestra at the Opera was accustomed to have things pretty much its own way—and partly through the sudden disappearance of Mademoiselle Cruvelli, the singer for whom the part of the Duchess Hélène had been written. This lady, who was the idol of the hour both in London and Paris, seems to have been unusually wilful even for a prima donna. Two years before she had disappointed her London admirers by suddenly disappearing in the height of the season and leaving all her engagements unfulfilled, and she now played the same trick upon the Parisians. After an absence of a month or two, during which the newspapers talked of nothing but the fugitive singer, she returned to the fold, and the new opera was forthwith put into study. In spite of its subject—the massacre of the French at Palermo (an odd choice, by the way, for an opera destined for the Parisian stage)—" Les Vêpres Siciliennes " was a great triumph. A

good deal of its success appears to have been
due to Mademoiselle Cruvelli, who exercised a
kind of fascination over the public of that day, for
after her retirement the opera was seldom given,
and seemed somehow to have lost much of its
power to charm. In Italy the licensing authorities
were staggered by so daring a subject, and the
opera had to be remodelled as "Giovanna di
Guzman," but it never achieved much success
in this shape : indeed these remodellings, which
Verdi had so often to put up with, seldom
seemed to succeed. "Les Vêpres Siciliennes"
contains much fine music, but apart from its
unwieldiness—it is in five long acts—it suffers
from the composer's conscious or unconscious
attempt to assimilate something of the grandiose
French style. It is by no means a typical work
of Verdi, and sounds far more old-fashioned now
than much of " Rigoletto."

1855 was decidedly one of Verdi's " Wander-
jahre," for, after being fêted in Paris, he paid a
flying visit to London, where "Il Trovatore" had
just been successfully produced.

The two things which seem most to have impressed him on this occasion were the Crystal Palace and Madame Viardot, whose performance of Azucena in " Il Trovatore " was certainly one of the most striking of her many fine impersonations. On his return to Italy Verdi set to work upon another opera— "Simon Boccanegra "—the *libretto* of which was compiled by the inevitable Piave from Schiller's " Fiesco." But the faithful librettist, who in " Rigoletto " and " La Traviata " had really surpassed himself, could make nothing of Schiller's tragedy. A distinguished Italian critic has confessed that six perusals of the " book " of " Simon Boccanegra " left him still in the dark as to what it was about ; so Englishmen may well be pardoned for finding it a trifle obscure. No music could succeed under such hopeless conditions, and " Simon Boccanegra " (produced at Venice in 1857) met with scanty favour. Twenty-four years later it was revived at Milan in a revised form. The *libretto* was touched up by Arrigo Boito, and

Verdi re-wrote some of his score for the occasion. Of that revival I shall speak in due course. "Aroldo," which was produced at Rimini in the same year, was merely a revised version of "Stiffelio." A new *libretto* had been written by Piave, but the music was for the most part unaltered. The Lutheran priest of "Stiffelio" was turned into a Saxon knight, and the scene of the opera was transferred to "il castello di Kenth" in England. The last Act, which was entirely new, takes place on the shores of Loch "Loomond." It contains a very fine storm scene, which in many of its details is worthy to be compared with the opening of "Otello," but even in its altered form the opera was never successful, and has long since been forgotten.

In his next work—"Un Ballo in Maschera"—Verdi scored one of the greatest successes of his career. The story was founded upon Scribe's "Gustave III.," but the Italian censors could not stomach the assassination of a king by one of his subjects, so the *locale* had to be changed to

America, and the Swedish monarch became the Governor of Boston. In France and England, however, the opera was often played in Italian dress, and the scene of the story transferred to Naples. This was principally done for the benefit of Signor Mario, who absolutely refused to don the Puritan costume of New England. "Un Ballo in Maschera" shows one side of Verdi's genius which he had hitherto been content to leave entirely in the background. The music of the page Oscar has a lightness, a grace, and a brilliancy which we may search for in vain in any of his earlier works. Since Verdi has given us "Falstaff" it is especially interesting to look back over the long series of his operas for traces of the extraordinary wealth of humour and fancy which was to burst out in the latest of his works. It is true that in his young days he wrote a comic opera—"Un Giorno di Regno"—but so far as can be judged from a perusal of the pianoforte score, there is very little in that early production which gave promise of the glories of "Falstaff."

It would be too much to say that " Un Ballo in Maschera" contains any actually humorous music, but it is a significant fact that after revelling in horrors throughout his career, he began in this work to appreciate the value of a lighter style of music, if only as a foil to the more tragic portions of his score. " Un Ballo in Maschera" is perhaps more than any of Verdi's operas associated with the name of Signor Mario. It was largely owing to the charm of his impersonation of Riccardo that the opera became so popular in England. Since his retirement the opera has gradually dropped out of the repertory. It has not been heard at Covent Garden since 1888, when M. Jean de Reszke and M. Lassalle appeared in it for the the first and only time in this country. Verdi's next work—" La Forza del Destino "—was commissioned by the Imperial Opera House at St. Petersburg. For the last time he had recourse to his faithful Piave. who produced a *libretto* founded upon a Spanish drama—" Don Alvar "—by Saavedra, which for sanguinary violence surpassed all his previous efforts. The last scene must really be a "record" in this way, including as it does two murders and a suicide. There is a certain amount of relief to all this battle, murder, and sudden death in the persons of a vivandière and a comic priest. The lighter parts of the opera are brilliant and effective, but have about as much to do with the story as the famous "underplot" of "The Critic." When "La Forza del Destino" was performed in Milan the *libretto* was revised and considerably abbreviated by Signor Ghislanzoni, and some alterations were introduced into the music, but out of Italy the opera has never been really successful.

In 1862 England had the honour of a third visit from the *maestro*. The Committee of the Universal Exhibition had commissioned four of the most famous composers of the day to write odes for the inauguration of the Exhibition. Sterndale Bennett represented England; Auber, France; Meyerbeer, Germany; and

Verdi, Italy. For some reason, which it is
scarcely worth while to investigate, Verdi's "Inno
delle Nazioni" was not performed at the opening Festival—indeed it was never heard within
the walls of the Exhibition itself at all. On the
24th of May it was performed in Her Majesty's
Theatre, the solo being sung by Mademoiselle
Tietjens. It is merely a *pièce d'occasion*, and is
certainly not likely ever to be heard again. It is
rather amusing to read a description of Verdi
as he appeared at this time to a partial and
probably feminine admirer : "A soft, thoughtful
face, mellow and olive-tinted ; cavernous eyes,
dreamy yet full of a subdued power, which hint
at the true artistic embers glowing steadily
behind ; an air of that romantic dignity, dashed
with a tone of melancholy which somehow fills
every Italian face ; a short, dark beard, trained
heart-shape, out of Titian or Pordenone; a spare
figure ; a stature over middle size. This is the
famous Giuseppe Verdi, the most popular composer in Europe."

In 1867 came the second French Exhibition,

and wishing once more to give lustre to their theatre by the production of a new work by the most famous of living musicians, the directors of the Académie Impériale de Musique applied to Verdi for a new opera. There was at first some idea of having "La Forza del Destino" translated, as it had not at that time been performed in Paris, but this scheme fell through, and Verdi set to work upon a libretto drawn by MM. Du Locle and Méry from Schiller's tragedy " Don Carlos." In spite of the *éclat* which attended its production on the 11th of March 1867, the success of the new opera was only moderate. The subject—the passion of the prince for his stepmother, Elizabeth of France—is by no means attractive, and the situations are for the most part commonplace or threadbare. The characters, too, are clumsily drawn and ineffectively grouped, and the end of the opera is unsatisfactory. The mysterious monk who saves Carlos from the Inquisitors is a quite unexplained enigma, and the ultimate fate of both hero and heroine is left

84

uncertain. The music of "Don Carlos" is exceedingly interesting to the student of Verdi's musical development, and much of it is intrinsically beautiful. Its faults are those of a work of transition. His old manner was beginning to lie heavily on Verdi's shoulders, but his genius was not yet ripe for the freer and clearer atmosphere of "Aida." Thus, while we find in "Don Carlos" many scenes of great beauty, such as the love-duet in the Third Act, and Elizabeth's "Stances" in the last Act, we are often pulled up short by some strange return to conventionalism. This might possibly have been no hindrance to its success if the *libretto* had not been so irredeemably dull. As it is, "Don Carlos" must be classed as one of Verdi's failures.

The history of the genesis of "Aida" is a curious one. In the first place, it was not written, as has so often been said, for the inauguration of Ismail Pacha's new Opera-house at Cairo, since the opening of the theatre dates from 1869. It was, however, written in response to a special request from the Khedive, who wished to enhance the glory of his theatre by the production of an opera dealing with an Egyptian subject. The question of terms was soon settled, for Verdi at once fell in love with the idea of an Egyptian opera, with its magnificent opportunities for local colour and novel dramatic effects. The original scheme of the plot is due to the fertile brain of Mariette Bey, the distinguished French Egyptologist. " Aida " is, in fact, founded upon an incident in Egyptian history with which Mariette had become acquainted in the course of his researches. The original sketch of the *libretto* was developed in French prose by M. Camille Du Locle, who worked under the eye of the composer at Busseto, and thus had the advantage of his advice and criticism. It was then translated into Italian verse by Signor Ghislanzoni. As a matter of fact, Verdi's share in the construction of the *libretto* was by no means an insignificant one. The idea of the last scene with its two stages, one above the other, was entirely due to him. When the score was finished, Verdi received a very pressing invitation to go to Cairo and superintend the production of his work. But his aversion to the sea was too strong for him, and he refused to leave Italy. Three times, indeed, he had braved the terrors of the English Channel, but the voyage to Egypt was a more serious affair, and the *maestro* decided to leave "Aida" in the hands of a trusty lieutenant, Signor Bottesini, well known in England as a phenomenal double-bass player and a composer of sacred music.

The production of "Aida" was delayed by many unforeseen circumstances, the chief of which was the siege of Paris. All the scenery and costumes had been designed and executed by various artists in the French capital, and though finished and packed for Cairo, they had to wait patiently until the capitulation released them. "Aida" was not, in fact, produced until December 24, 1871. The Cairene theatre was crowded to its utmost by one of the most varied audiences ever packed between four

87

walls. Side by side with journalists from
Paris and Milan sat Copts and Arabians, Greek
merchants, English pleasure-seekers, and *dilettanti* from all parts of the world. The Khedive
honoured the performance with his presence,
and three boxes on the second tier, thickly
veiled in white muslin, contained the ladies of
the harem.

In " Aida " Verdi had the advantage of one of
the best *libretti* ever written. To what use he
turned it all the world knows. At first the general
opinion was that he had come under the influence
of Wagner ; even so sane and clear-headed a critic
as M. Ernest Reyer thought the new work "atteint
de germanisme." However, in the seventies
everything that was not a mere string of couplets
and cavatinas was put down as Wagnerian. The
world had not then found out the difference between a leading motive and a repeated motive.
The latter had been a favourite with Verdi for
long. It is at any rate as old as " Il Trovatore,"
and in " Aida " he uses it from time to time
with striking effect. To those who knew their

Verdi well, the leap from "Don Carlos" to "Aida" was not so great after all, and though the lesser fry filled the air with shrieks about Wagnerism and denationalisation and so forth, the wiser men knew that Verdi's new style was only the logical development of what had gone before. The subject of "Aida," so remote from the ordinary operatic groove, no doubt tempted him to a fresher and more vivid realism, and the possibilities of Egyptian local colour must have opened a new world to so consummate a master of orchestration. Local colour is too often a dangerous stumbling-block to musicians. The path of musical progress is strewn with the corpses of Oriental operas. The late Mr. Carl Rosa knew this well enough, and in his later days, taught by sad experience, would never look at an opera on an Eastern subject. But where all the world had failed, Verdi scored his most brilliant success. The temple scene in the first act of "Aida" is perhaps the finest example of local colour judiciously applied that the history of opera can show. The two melodies which are used in this scene are genuine Oriental tunes, but by his dexterous treatment of them Verdi has made them entirely his own. Another noble scene is the judgment of Rhadames in the last act, a page of extraordinary dramatic power. The third act shows the lyrical side of Verdi's genius in its most voluptuous aspect. There is an exotic charm about his picture of the Isle of Philae and the moonlit Nile, which it is impossible to convey in words. "Aida" has its exaggerations and vulgarities, but such scenes as these must ensure its immortality. Its success was enormous, and shows at present not a sign of diminution.

To this period belongs Verdi's one contribution to Chamber Music, a String Quartet, which was written at Naples in 1873. Verdi had gone thither to superintend the production of "Aida," but the sudden illness of one of the singers delayed the rehearsals, and the composer employed his enforced leisure in writing his Quartet. Verdi's genius was not at ease in the shackles of the quartet-form, and the work is only valuable

as a curiosity. It was performed at the Popular
Concerts in 1876.

In 1868, after the death of Rossini, Verdi
had conceived the idea of honouring the memory
of the great composer by the performance of a
Requiem Mass which should be written in
concert by the leading musicians of Italy. The
text of the Mass was divided into thirteen portions, which were distributed among thirteen
composers. Verdi reserved the last movement,
the "Libera me," for himself, presumably thinking that, as the undoubted head of the Italian
school of music, he had a right to the last word.
The thirteen *maestri* all came up to time with
their movements, but the result was such an
indescribable hotch-potch that the idea of per
forming the Requiem was at once felt to be out
of the question. Some years afterwards, Alessandro Manzoni, the famous poet and novelist,
died at Milan. He was regarded with the
greatest possible affection and respect by the
whole of Italy, and to the Milanese, with whom
he had made his home for many years, he was an

ITALIAN MUSICAL COMPOSERS

object of positive adoration. Verdi had been
united to Manzoni by bonds of the tenderest
sympathy, and he at once offered to compose a
Requiem, which should be performed in one of
the churches of Milan upon the anniversary of
the great poet's death. The Municipality of
Milan accepted his offer with alacrity, and the
Mass, of which the original " Libera me " formed
the nucleus, was performed for the first time in
the Church of San Marco on the 22nd of May
1874. So deep an impression was made by the
new work that three further performances were
given in the Teatro alla Scala, the first of
which was conducted by Verdi in person. One
week later the Requiem was given at the Opéra
Comique in Paris. Here, too, its success was
something prodigious, and since then it has
been repeatedly performed in every quarter of
the globe. England alone has remained cold
to the beauties of this noble work. Critics,
indeed, are no longer blind to its greatness. It is no longer the fashion to dismiss
it with a word as sensuous or theatrical, or to

92

point with pedantic rapture to the fact that some kapellmeister or other found fifty or a hundred, or five hundred grammatical mistakes in the score. But the great public will have none of it. At the last London performance, that given by the Bach Choir in December 1892, St. James's Hall presented a most doleful array of empty benches. English conservatism, true to Handelian tradition, will not tolerate sacred music which differs from the established model. It is a distressing fact—and the most devoted admirers of Handel, of whom I am one, must with sorrow admit it—that Handel's popularity has been the destruction of musical taste in England. The average English concert-goer takes the " Messiah " as his standard, and everything that he cannot gauge by this measure he consigns at once to perdition.

After launching the " Requiem " Verdi retired to his property at Sant' Agata, and there for many years lived the quiet life of an ordinary country gentleman. It seemed as though music had been finally banished from his thoughts, and as time went on the world taught itself to believe that his career had closed once and for all. In 1865 he had written to a friend: "At Sant' Agata we never make music, nor talk about it, and you will run the risk of finding a piano not only out of tune, but without strings." This may have been literally true; at any rate, for many years the fields and farm of his country estate, his stables and his paddocks, seemed to have compensated the aged *maestro* for the whirl and bustle of the theatre and the pomps and glories of his earlier years. In 1881, it is true, the revival of "Simon Boccanegra" drew him for a moment from his retirement. The failure of this opera in 1857 had been a disappointment to Verdi. He felt that its want of success was largely due to the weakness of the *libretto.* So, in view of its performance at La Scala he called in the assistance of Arrigo Boito, the famous poet-composer, and between them they subjected the work to a complete overhauling. Boito re-wrote some of the *libretto* and altered a good deal of the remainder, and

Verdi not only revised his score, but orchestrated it afresh from start to finish, and wrote
some entirely new music, including the magnificent *finale* to the first Act, one of the noblest
pieces he has ever penned, worthy in every
respect of the mature glories of "Otello." The
success of "Simon Boccanegra" at Milan was
very great, and was not a little due to the very
remarkable impersonation of the Doge by M.
Victor Maurel. Two years later, when the great
baritone took the Théâtre des Nations in Paris
for a season of Italian Opera, he opened his
campaign with "Simon Boccanegra." But
although the cast was a very strong one, including Madame Fidès-Devriès and M. Edouard de
Reszke, the opera was coldly received, and was
performed only eight times. In England it has
never been heard. In its present form, indeed,
it is rather a curious mixture of Verdi's earlier
and later styles, and the music which he wrote
for its revival makes what is left of the original
work seem doubly old-fashioned. But though
the world is not likely to hear more of "Simon

Boccanegra," the revival is an important landmark in the history of Verdi's development, for
it introduced Boito to him in the character of
librettist, and laid the foundations of "Otello"
and "Falstaff."

In the making of an opera, as in everything
else, two heads are better than one. Boito is
not only a poet of acknowledged excellence, but
also a musician of high attainment and an acute
critic. His labours, we may be sure, did not
cease when he handed to Verdi the poems of
"Otello" and "Falstaff," the two finest *libretti*
in existence. Indeed his influence is very
apparent in both scores, particularly in that of
"Otello." In speaking of Verdi's two later
works, so admirably concise and dramatic, one
cannot help thinking with a sigh of Wagner
and his portentous dramas, and wishing that
he too had had a Boito at his elbow, armed
with a judicious pruning-knife. We should
not then have had to submit to the ruthless
mutilations which in every theatre, except the
Festspielhaus at Bayreuth, disguise and detract

from the beauties of the German master's lyric dramas.

It was not very long after the revival of "Simon Boccanegra" that the world of music was delighted with the rumour of a new opera from Verdi's pen. In those days it was spoken of as "Iago." Verdi was reluctant at first to call his work by a name which had already been used by Rossini. But the earlier composer's work had for many years disappeared from the stage, and in the end it was decided that the new opera should be known as "Otello." The opera was produced at Milan on the 5th of February 1887, with a success that can only be described as overwhelming. Critics and musicians had assembled from all parts of the world, and the verdict, at any rate among those *che sanno*, was unanimous. Modest as he is, Verdi had for once to give himself up to the wild enthusiasm which prevailed, and to consent to be fêted as surely never composer had been fêted before.

In writing of "Otello" and "Falstaff" I find it difficult to avoid terms which may appear extravagant. I frankly confess to an admiration for these two works which borders upon idolatry. They seem to me to embody all the best features of the modern school of music without for a moment losing touch with the great masters of the past, and to show once and for all that it is possible to combine absolute truth of declamation with a stream of the richest and most characteristic melody.

Verdi had in Boito, as I have already said, a coadjutor the value of whose assistance can scarcely be over-estimated. The *libretto* of "Otello" alone would suffice to stamp him a poet of unusual excellence. In the most masterly manner he contrived to compress the entire tragedy into four scenes, without omitting one point of real importance to the plot. There are only two episodes in his poem which find no counterpart in Shakespeare, and it is hardly too much to say that they are in every way worthy of their surroundings. One is the delightful chain of choruses in the second act, in which the Cypriote fishermen bring their gifts

to Desdemona, an incident of simple grace and
gaiety which throws the tragic conclusion of the
act into lurid relief; the other is the famous
" Credo," Iago's terrible confession of unfaith,
in which, amidst a pandemonium of mordant
shakes and crashing brass, he lays bare the
inmost recesses of his soul. All the rest is pure
Shakespeare. Occasionally Boito has contrived
with incomparable address to transfer lines and
phrases from one scene to another, notably in
the duet at the conclusion of the first act, into
which is incorporated some of the famous speech
before the Senate.

I will not attempt an elaborate analysis of
either *libretto* or music, because every musician
knows, or should know, both by heart already,
and the outside world cares but little for such
disquisitions. But I will indicate as well as I
can some points in the score which show the
great advance Verdi made in " Otello " beyond
all his previous work. In every one of his
operas since " Rigoletto " there is something to
admire. " Aida " in particular is a work of

99

superb power and beauty ; but before the days of " Otello " Verdi seemed scarcely to have his genius under complete control. He had melody, passion, and colour at his command, but his power of character-drawing was as yet not fully developed. It is not until we reach " Otello " that we find him in command of that subtle power which, in half-a-dozen notes, apparently thrown together by accident, is able to reveal the soul of a man as plainly as though his character were discussed upon a printed page. It is possible that in my admiration for " Otello " I may sometimes read in Verdi's music a meaning which he did not intend to convey. This is a failing to which commentators are peculiarly liable, and the great ones of this world—authors as well as musicians—suffer from it at times. Shakespeare is already half stifled by the elucidations of his admirers, and it is possible that my enthusiasm for Verdi may occasionally tempt me to trespass in the same way.

There are only two principal characters in " Otello," for Desdemona is of a negative rather

than of a positive cast of mind, and Emilia and
Cassio are merely thumb-nail sketches. But
Othello and Iago are of supreme importance,
and upon them Verdi has lavished the utmost
resources of his genius. There is an exquisite
art shown in the means used to introduce them
to the audience. We see them first precisely as
they appeared to the casual onlooker, Othello a
victorious general, flushed with his triumph over
the Turks, Iago a bluff soldier, with a dash of
cynicism (he says himself, " Io non sono che un
critico "), and a hearty companion over a bottle.
With his friend and hanger-on, Rodrigo, he does
not mind showing a little more of his true
nature, but before the others he is "honest Iago"
to the backbone. After the duel we get fresh
light upon both characters. Othello's entrance
is dignified and his first utterance has all the
grandeur of a born ruler. Suddenly Montano's
" Son ferito" rouses him. His wild outburst
" Pel cielo, già il sangue mio ribolle," affords us
a glimpse of the barbarian concealed under a
courtly exterior. It is only a glimpse, but it

gives us some inkling of the wild passions lurking beneath a veneer of self-command.

Iago's share in this scene is very important. It shows us for the first time the ancient's attitude to his general. Iago had evidently gauged Othello's power of penetration. With the Moor he knew that he could safely broaden his effects, and in his account of the riot his assumption of guileless honesty is exaggerated even to the borders of the grotesque. No one but Othello could possibly have been deceived by the ridiculous fervour of his " Avessi primo stroncati i piè che qui m'addusser." The duet which closes the act, apart from its manifold poetic and melodic beauties, throws an important light upon the character of Othello's love. We see that his passion for Desdemona has carried him to the verge of uxoriousness. There is a subtle art in this, for without it we could scarcely believe in the sudden and terrible growth of jealousy in the next act.

With the opening of the second act, Iago reveals himself in his true colours. The famous

"Credo" leaves not a corner of his soul un-
explored. After this we know the man in all
his terrors, and watch his course through the
tragedy with a spell-bound horror. Othello's
entrance is the signal for a scene, which, though
it may not appeal to the groundlings, is perhaps
the noblest instance in the opera of Verdi's
mastery of dialogue. Every word tells, because
every word is fitted to exactly the right note.
The orchestral portion of this scene is comparatively unimportant, but there are touches
here and there which reveal the hand of a
master. As Iago whispers his venomous
suspicions, the music seems dimly to suggest
the writhing of some loathsome reptile. When
at length Othello sees the drift of Iago's hints
and suggestions his rage bursts forth with fearful
energy. There is an unholy triumph in Iago's
terrible counsel, " Temete, signor, la gelosia," set
to a harsh progression of consecutive fifths, and
we feel all the misery of Othello's tempest-tossed
soul in his one cry of " Miseria mia."

Throughout this scene and that which may be

regarded as its pendant at the close of the act, Verdi's power of characterisation is triumphantly displayed. Othello's almost child-like ingenuousness is wonderfully indicated by such subtle touches as the pathetic "Quel fazzoletto io li diedi, pegno primo d'amor," while the true greatness of his soul is revealed in the poignant anguish of his farewell to glory, "Ora e per sempre addio." It would be superfluous to point out the beauties of such well-known passages as Iago's tale of Cassio's dream, or his terrible description of jealousy, "E un' idra fosca," a veritable musical embodiment of the green-eyed monster, or the magnificent close of the act, in which, after his maniacal cry of "Sangue, sangue," Othello calls upon the marble heaven to witness his vengeance. These are beauties which, even at the first hearing, could not fail to strike any intelligent listener.

There is a sinister calm about the third act. Before the curtain has risen we hear the terrible "idra fosca" writhing in the orchestra, and there is a gloom about Othello's words and manner

in the opening scene which seems to presage
the fatal deed he is meditating. The irony of
Othello's reception of Desdemona is hit off with
a happy touch, and throughout the magnificent
duet which follows there are passages of extraordinary beauty. At one point the passionate
pleading of his wife almost melts Othello's iron
purpose. The music seems to rock in uncertainty, but the moment passes, and he dashes her
from him. The following scene is a counterpart
to the *addio* of the second act. That was a
farewell to glory; this is a farewell to love.
Blank anguish has surely never been painted in
colours so dreary and hopeless as the minor
passage with which it opens, nor would it be
easy to find a parallel to the passionate grief of
the *cantabile*. There comes a gleam of light
upon the scene in the famous Handkerchief Trio,
a passage of extreme delicacy and grace. In
more ways than one it foreshadows the methods
of " Falstaff," not less in its brilliant vivacity
than in its almost symphonic structure. The
elaborate *finale* which closes the act is founded

upon three melodies of exquisite beauty, but it nevertheless sounds stiff and conventional after what has gone before, until we reach Othello's furious outburst, " Fuggite," which disperses the assembled company in terror and leaves the stage to Iago and himself. The close of this act is one of Boito's triumphs. Nothing could be less conventional or at the same time more dramatic than the final tableau. The senseless form of Othello lies prostrate beneath his persecutor's foot, while the joyous cries of the crowd outside the palace throw into lurid relief the concentrated malevolence of Iago's scornful cry, " Ecco il Leone." It is Æschylean in its simplicity and force. In the last act, apart from the admirable conciseness which makes it a model for future generations, the musical in- terest centres in Desdemona's exquisite Willow Song and " Ave Maria," in the passionate grief of her farewell to Emilia, so curiously remini- scent of a famous passage in " La Traviata," and in the exquisite echo of the love-duet which brings the opera to a conclusion.

The secret of "Falstaff" was well kept. Not a breath of rumour had even suggested the possibility of a new opera from Verdi's pen, until at a supper-party in Milan, at which the composer and his wife and various members of the firm of Ricordi were present, Boito suddenly proposed the health of the fat knight. Even then no one quite knew what he was driving at. After a little more mystification the collaborators deigned to explain. Boito had drawn another of his incomparable *libretti* from Shakespeare. This time "The Merry Wives of Windsor" had been laid under contribution, together with one or two extracts from "Henry IV." It was pure comedy throughout, and the music was already half written. The news spread over Europe like wild-fire. Every one was delighted to hear that Verdi had again taken pen in hand, but opinions were divided as to his choice of subject. Was the man, who all his life long had revelled in tragedy, if not melodrama, able to treat a comic subject with the requisite lightness? Could the musician of "Otello" give us the ideal

" Falstaff " ? All doubts were set at rest on the 12th of March 1893, when " Falstaff " was pro- duced at the Teatro alla Scala at Milan, before an audience of musicians and critics assembled from the length and breadth of Europe. Never in the history of music has the verdict of critics been so absolutely unanimous as in the case of " Falstaff." From those who know, or even pretend to know, anything about music not one word of detraction has yet been heard. It is almost safe to say, as has been said in the domain of poetry of Milton's " Lycidas," that the power of appre- ciating " Falstaff " may be taken as the outward and visible sign of a cultivated musical taste. The *libretto* is an almost miraculous example of Boito's knack of condensation. The first act shows us Falstaff despatching his letters to Mistress Ford and Mistress Page, and their plot to circumvent him. In the second we have his visit to Mistress Ford, his concealment in the buck-basket, and his lamentable exit through the window into the Thames, and the last act shows us his final discomfiture in Windsor Forest.

Several important incidents and a good many minor characters are left out, and some of those which are retained are slightly modified, but the result is a model of conciseness and lucidity. Italian critics have objected that the language is sometimes unnecessarily and even anachronistically archaic, but as to this an Englishman cannot pretend to be a competent judge. At any rate, there is nothing archaic about the music, which is the very incarnation of youth and high spirits. It goes with a laugh from beginning to end. One or two critics have tried with questionable success to exalt " Falstaff" by depreciating " Otello," principally upon the grounds of the composer's treatment of the orchestra, which they assert to be more "symphonic" in the later work. Such comparisons are as a rule elusive, especially in the case of a tragedy and comedy. Whether the orchestra is to be treated symphonically or not must surely depend upon what is happening upon the stage. So long as one situation remains unchanged upon the stage, as for instance the interview between Dr. Caius, Bardolph, Pistol and Falstaff with which "Falstaff' opens, then a symphonic treatment of the orchestra—that is to say, a development of one or two themes at some length—is no doubt advisable, because a general impression of the situation is all that it is necessary to convey, and the declamation may be left more or less to take care of itself; but a symphonic treatment of such a scene as the first dialogue between Othello and Iago in the second act of "Otello" would be a grievous artistic mistake, because here every word is of the utmost importance, and the orchestra must not be allowed to distract our attention for a moment from the declamation. But, when occasion demands it, Verdi can be symphonic enough even in "Otello" to satisfy the most fastidious critic; witness the Handkerchief Trio, in which the orchestra is working away at one theme almost the whole time.

Besides, "Falstaff" is very well able to stand upon its own merits without any injudicious support of this kind. Even to those who knew

their Verdi best—perhaps in fact to them most
of all—the music came as a revelation. The
rollicking humour which pervades the whole
score, the flashing wit, the exquisite snatches of
tenderness, which come for a moment as a relief
to the almost perennial flow of high spirits, make
up a whole to parallel which we must go back
to the days of Mozart. The character of
Falstaff naturally dominates the scene, and upon
him Verdi has concentrated the lens of his
genius. The leading note of his character is
sublime self-conceit. If his belief in himself
were shattered, he would be merely a vulgar
sensualist and debauchee. As it is, he is a hero.
For one terrible moment in the last act his self-
satisfaction wavers. He looks round and sees
every one laughing at him. Can it be that he
has been made a fool of? But no, he puts the
horrible suggestion from him, and in a flash is
himself again. "Son io" he exclaims with a
triumphant inspiration, "che vi fa scaltri, l'arguzia
mia crea l'arguzia degl' altri." Verdi has caught
this touch and indeed a hundred others through-

out the opera with astonishing truth and delicacy. Ford too is very happily hit off. The contrast between the jealous irascibility of his real character and the fatuous folly which he assumes in the disguise of Fontana is brought out to the life. His great monologue is a wonderful piece of declamation. It is a worthy counterpart to the " Credo " in Otello.

There is one character which neither Boito nor Verdi has fully realised. Their Pistol is a mere shadow. No one who loves " The Merry Wives " can help feeling a pang of regret that the immortal Ancient's delightful mock-heroics should be so ruthlessly expunged. Probably Boito's idea was to give greater prominence to the protagonist, and dramatically he was very likely right, but it is rather a shock—one instance will serve—to find Pistol's answer to Falstaff's inquiries about Ford reduced to a bald " Si " in place of the famous " I ken the wight ; he is of substance good."

Boito has taken a poet's licence with Page and excised him completely, together with several other less important characters. "Sweet Anne Page" becomes Nannetta Ford, but otherwise remains true to Shakespeare. Her dainty little love-scenes with Fenton are indescribably fresh and delightful. In the opening of the last act the composer strikes a deeper note than at any other point in the drama. There is an unearthly charm about this scene which is new to students of Verdi, a kind of *clair de lune* effect quite unlike anything he has given to the world before. After the exuberant humours of the second act the calm serenity of the sleeping forest seems doubly impressive. The whole scene strikingly recalls the moonlit street and the sleepy watchman of "Die Meistersinger." We have here, too, an admirable opportunity of comparing the early Verdi with the later. In the last act of "Rigoletto" there is an aggressive demon of a clock, which rattles off the strokes of midnight in a business-like but notably unimpressive manner. How different it is in "Falstaff." Round the twelve strokes of midnight Verdi has woven a halo of dim and mysterious chords, which breathe the very atmosphere of mystery and romance. All the charm of fairyland seems transmuted into sound; indeed all the fairy music is delicate and ethereal in the highest degree. Nothing so full of imaginative beauty or so thoroughly imbued with the true romantic spirit has been written since the days of Weber.

Perhaps the most wonderful thing about "Falstaff" is the fact that it was written by a man eighty years old. It seems to breathe the spirit of youth in every bar. Complicated as the part-writing often is, the most elaborate concerted pieces flow on as naturally as a ballad. Verdi says he thoroughly enjoyed writing it, and one can well believe it. He has combined the grace and science of a Mozart with the high spirits of a schoolboy. The glorious fugue with which the opera ends is a type of the whole work. It is as learned as possible. Inversions, pedal-point, *stretto*, all are there, but not a whiff of the lamp. All is pure fun and merriment. If "Falstaff" should prove—which may the Muses forefend—to be Verdi's farewell to the world, he will at least, like Rembrandt in his latest portrait, have taken leave of it with a smile on his face.

Unlike his great contemporary Wagner, Verdi knows nothing of the *cacoëthes scribendi*. He has always been a man of few words, and those who wish to know his artistic creed must look for it in the pages of his operas. One of his utterances, however, deserves to be widely known ; indeed, I would have it printed in letters of gold upon the walls of every Academy of Music in the world. It is a letter which he wrote to Signor Florimo in 1871, refusing the post of Director of the Conservatoire at Naples, which had become vacant through the death of Mercadante :

GENOA, *January 5th*, 1871.

DEAREST FLORIMO,

Nothing could be more flattering to my vanity than the invitation to be Director of the Conservatoire at Naples, which you have conveyed to me from the Committee and so many

distinguished musicians of your city. I am
deeply pained that I cannot reply to it as I
could have wished, but my occupations, my
habits and my love of independence, all forbid
me to undertake so grave a responsibility. But
how about Art, you will say? Well, I have done
what I could, and if in the future I am to do
anything more, my time must be completely my
own. If it were not so, I hope you will believe
that I should have been proud to have filled the
post held in former times by Alessandro Scarlatti, Durante and Leo, the founders of your
school. So far from looking upon it as deroga-
tory, I should have considered it an honour to
lead the rising generation in the steps of those
famous masters. I should have desired, so to
speak, to put one foot upon the past and the
other upon the present and future, for the
" music of the future " has no terrors for me. I
should have said to my scholars: "Practise fugue
steadily and perseveringly, until you have the
mere grammar of your art at your finger-ends.
You will accustom yourselves in this way to take

a firm grasp of your subject, you will acquire a
sound, vigorous method of part-writing, and you
will learn how to modulate without affectation.
Study Palestrina and a few of his contemporaries,
then skip to Marcello, and give your special
attention to his treatment of recitative. Go now
and then to performances of modern operas, but
do not allow yourselves to be dazzled by their
harmonic and orchestral brilliancy. Do not be
led astray either by the chord of the diminished
seventh, which is the curse of modern music.
Many of our composers now-a-days cannot write
four bars without using it half-a-dozen times.
Do not neglect your literary studies. No
composer is worth his salt who is not at the
same time a man of wide culture." When all
their studies are completed, I should say at last
to the youngsters : " Now put your hands on
your hearts. Write and (given the artistic temperament) you will be composers. At any rate,
you will not swell the crowd of imitators and
of well-meaning folk who are ever seeking and
never finding. For singers I should insist upon

the study of the ancients together with modern declamation. Easy as these maxims seem, you would find that twelve months of the year would not be enough to teach them as they should be taught. Everything that I have in the world, house, interests, fortune, all combine to keep me here. I am only human: can you ask me to give them up? Be so kind, then, my dear Florimo, as to convey my very great regret to your colleagues and to the musicians of your beautiful Naples. Since I cannot accept the honour you offer me, I pray that you may find a Director who is above all a learned man and a martinet. Licences and contrapuntal errors are all very well in a theatre; sometimes they are not only admissible but admirable, but in an Academy—never. Turn to the antique and it will be an advance. Farewell.

Believe me always,

Yours most affectionate,

GIUSEPPE VERDI.

It is perhaps impossible to leave Verdi
without touching upon the comparisons which
have been made between him and Wagner,
and the question as to how far the German
master's influence may have affected the
remarkable development of the Italian. Additional point is given to the discussion by
the fact that each composer has written only
one comic opera, for Verdi's early effort—
" Un Giorno di Regno "—may for all practical
purposes be conveniently disregarded. " Die
Meistersinger," it is true, is not a comic
opera in the same sense as " Falstaff." It has
a far deeper human interest, apart from the
question of a lofty symbolic meaning which
ardent Wagnerians have extracted from its
pages. But even were the scope of the two
works far more similar than it actually is, a
comparison of the two would still be an
unfruitful task, for they are constructed upon
totally diverse systems. With Wagner the Leit-
Motiv is all-important, and as a consequence
the polyphonic treatment of the orchestra is

the hinge upon which the whole work turns. The centre of Verdi's system is the human voice, and he uses the orchestra mainly as an accompaniment. It would be easy, I know, to point out instances in "Die Meistersinger" in which the instrumental part of the score is subordinated to vocal melody, and there are many passages in "Falstaff" where the principal interest lies in the treatment of the orchestra. There are exceptions to every rule; but what I have said indicates the general lines upon which each composer went to work. Are we, then, to suppose that Verdi owed nothing to Wagner? It would be dangerous to affirm that he has never read " Lohengrin," or, if he has done so, that he was not deeply impressed by its manifold beauties; but this, I think, can safely be said, that such a development as Verdi's is not in the nature of things impossible, even if we presuppose no external influence whatsoever. If Gluck could rise from "Artamene" to "Orfeo," Rossini from "Semiramide" to "Guillaume Tell," or Meyer-

beer from " Il Crociato " to " Les Huguenots,"
why should Verdi need a Wagner to help him
over the gulf from " Rigoletto " to " Aida," or
from " Aida " to " Falstaff " ? I look upon the
evolution of Verdi's genius as one of the grand
and gradual processes of Nature. There is no
need to invoke the help of a hothouse to
explain the passage of a flower from bud to
blossom. Verdi is complete in himself. The
germ of " Falstaff " lay buried in " Oberto." It
needed only the fostering power of time to bring
it to maturity.

It is early yet to speak of Verdi's probable
influence upon posterity. The production of
two such works as " Otello " and " Falstaff "
can scarcely be without influence upon subsequent Italian music, but, strictly speaking,
Verdi is hardly the man to found a school.
He is not one of the world's great revolu-
tionists, like Monteverde, Gluck, or Wagner.
His genius lies not in overturning systems and
exploring untrodden paths, but in developing
existing materials to the highest conceivable

pitch of beauty and completeness. His music
is not the product of deliberate theory. It is
the voice of Nature speaking in the idiom of
Art.

Of Verdi's career since the production of
" Falstaff" there is little to be said. He
continues to astonish the world with such
proofs of his unwearied diligence and activity
as are embodied in visits to Paris to superintend the rehearsals of " Falstaff "and " Otello."
For the production of the latter he was
induced by the directors of the Académie de
Musique to write a short ballet which was introduced into the *finale* of the third act. The new
music was scarcely worthy of the composer and
harmonised very badly with its surroundings.
The idea of a ballet in " Otello," was a grievous
mistake, and it is to be regretted that Verdi
should for once have allowed his good nature
to prevail over his sense of artistic propriety.
As regards the future nothing is certainly
known. There have been rumours of a " King
Lear," a " Romeo and Juliet," a " Richard

III.," and lastly, of an "Ugolino"; but, if there is any truth in these reports, the secret has not been divulged. One thing is certain, that nothing is needed to complete the glory of this astonishing man, and if he chose in his eighty-second year to have done finally with music and things musical, however much we might regret his determination, we could scarcely venture to be surprised at it.

THE PUBLISHED WORKS OF VERDI

DRAMATIC WORKS

A chronological list giving the names of the singers at the original production of each opera and at the first performance in the British Islands.

OBERTO, CONTE DI SAN BONIFACIO

MILAN, *November 17th,* 1839

Leonora .	. Signora Raineri-Marini.
Cuniza .	. Mrs. Alfred Shaw.
Riccardo	. Signor Salvi.
Oberto .	. Signor Marini.

UN GIORNO DI REGNO

MILAN, *September 5th,* 1840

La Marchesa del Poggio .	Signora Raineri-Marini.
Giulietta .	Signora Abbadia.
Edoardo .	. Signor Salvi.
Belfiore .	. Signor Ferlotti.

GIUSEPPE VERDI

NABUCODONOSOR

MILAN, *March 9th*, 1842

Abigaele .	. Signora Strepponi.
Fenena . .	. Signora Bellinzaghi.
Ismaele . .	Signor Miraglia.
Nabucodonosor	. Signor Ronconi.
Zaccaria	Signor Dérivis.

LONDON, *March 3rd*, 1846

Abigaele .	. Signora Sanchioli.
Fenena	Signora Corbari.
Idaspe	Signor Corelli.
Nino . .	Signor Fornasari.
Orotaspe	Signor Botelli.

I LOMBARDI ALLA PRIMA CROCIATA

MILAN, *February 11th*, 1843

Giselda . . .	. Signora Frezzolini.
Oronte . . .	. Signor Guasco.
Arvino . . .	. Signor Severi.
Pagano . . .	. Signor Dérivis.

LONDON, *May 12th*, 1846

Giselda . .	. Signora Grisi.
Oronte . .	Signor Mario.
Arvino . . .	. Signor Corelli.
Pagano . . .	. Signor Fornasari

125

ITALIAN MUSICAL COMPOSERS

ERNANI

VENICE, *March* 9th, 1844

Elvira	Madame Löwe.
Ernani	Signor Guasco.
Don Carlo . . .	Signor Superchi.
Silva	Signor Selva.

LONDON, *March* 8th, 1845

Elvira	Signora Borio.
Ernani . .	Signor Moriani.
Don Carlo . .	Signor Botelli.
Silva . . .	Signor Fornasari.

I DUE FOSCARI

ROME, *November* 3rd, 1844

Lucrezia	Signora Barbieri-Nini.
Jacopo	Signor Roppa.
Francesco . . .	Signor De Bassini.

LONDON, *April* 10th, 1847.

Lucrezia	Madame Montenegro.
Jacopo	Signor Fraschini.
Francesco . . .	Signor Coletti.

GIOVANNA D'ARCO

MILAN, *February* 15th, 1845

Giovanna . . .	Signora Frezzolini.
Carlo VII. . .	Signor Poggi.
Giacomo . .	Signor Colini.

GIUSEPPE VERDI

ALZIRA

NAPLES, *August 12th*, 1845

Alzira . . . . Signora Tadolini.
Zamoro . . . Signor Fraschini.
Gusmano . . . Signor Coletti.

ATTILA

VENICE, *March 17th*, 1846

Odabella . . Madame Sophie Löwe.
Foresto . . . Signor Guasco.
Ezio . . . . Signor Costantini.
Attila . . . . Signor Marini.

LONDON, *March 14th*, 1848

Odabella . . . Mademoiselle Cruvelli.
Foresto . . . Signor Gardoni.
Ezio . . . . Signor Cuzzani.
Attila . . . Signor Belletti.

MACBETH

FLORENCE, *March 14th*, 1847

Lady Macbeth . . Signora Barbieri-Nini.
Macduff . . . Signor Brunacci.
Macbeth . . . Signor Varesi.
Banquo . . . Signor Benedetti.

127

ITALIAN MUSICAL COMPOSERS

DUBLIN, *March 30th*, 1859

Lady Macbeth	. . Madame Viardot.
Macduff	. . . Signor Corsi.
Macbeth	. . . Signor Graziani.
Banquo	. . . Signor Lanzoni.

I MASNADIERI

LONDON, *July 22nd*, 1847

Amalia .	. . . Madame Jenny Lind.
Carlo .	. . . Signor Gardoni.
Francesco	. . . Signor Coletti.
Maximilian .	. . Signor Lablache.

IL CORSARO

TRIESTE, *October 25th*, 1848

Medora	. . . Signora Barbieri-Nini.
Gulnare	. . . Signora Rampazzini.
Corrado	. . . Signor Fraschini.
Seide .	. . . Signor De Bassini.

LA BATTAGLIA DI LEGNANO

ROME, *January 27th*, 1849

Lida	. . . Signora De Giuli.
Arrigo	. . Signor Fraschini.
Rolando	. . . Signor Colini.

GIUSEPPE VERDI

LUISA MILLER

NAPLES, *December 8th*, 1849

Luisa	Signora Gazzaniga.
La Duchessa . . .	Signora Salandri.
Rodolfo	Signor Malvezzi.
Miller . .	Signor De Bassini.
Walter	Signor Arati.
Wurm	Signor Selva.

LONDON, *January 8th*, 1853

Luisa	Mdlle. Piccolomini.
La Duchessa . .	Madame Alboni.
Rodolfo . . .	Signor Giuglini.
Miller	Signor Beneventano.
Walter	Signor Vialetti.
Wurm	Signor Castelli.

STIFFELIO

TRIESTE, *November 16th*, 1850

Lina	Signora Gazzaniga.
Stiffelio	Signor Fraschini.
Stankar	Signor Colini.
Raffaele	Signor Raineri.

RIGOLETTO

VENICE, *March 11th*, 1851

Gilda	Signora Brambilla.
Maddalena . . .	Signora Casaloni.
Il Duca	Signor Miraté.
Rigoletto	Signor Varesi.
Sparafucile . . .	Signor Pons.

ITALIAN MUSICAL COMPOSERS

LONDON, May 14th, 1853

Gilda	Madame Bosio.
Maddalena	Madame Nantier-Didiée.
Il Duca	Signor Mario.
Rigoletto	Signor Ronconi.
Sparafucile	Signor Tagliafico.

IL TROVATORE

ROME, January 19th, 1853

Leonora	Signora Penco.
Azucena	Signora Goggi.
Manrico	Signor Boucardé.
Conte di Luna	Signor Guicciardi.

LONDON, May 10th, 1855

Leonora	Mdlle. Ney.
Azucena	Madame Viardot.
Manrico	Signor Tamberlik.
Conte di Luna	Signor Graziani.

LA TRAVIATA

VENICE, March 6th, 1853

Violetta	Signora Salvini-Donatelli
Alfredo	Signor Graziani.
Germont	Signor Varesi.

LONDON, May 28th, 1856

Violetta	Mdlle. Piccolomini.
Alfredo	Signor Calzolari.
Germont	Signor Beneventano.

GIUSEPPE VERDI

LES VÊPRES SICILIENNES
PARIS, *June* 13th, 1855

Hélène	Mdlle. Cruvelli.
Ninette	Madame Sannier.
Henri	M. Gueymard.
Procida	M. Bonnehée.
Montfort	M. Obin.

LONDON, *July* 27th, 1859

Hélène	Mdlle. Tietjens.
Ninette	Mdlle. Dell' Anese.
Henri . . .	Signor Mongini.
Procida	Signor Vialetti.
Montfort . . .	Signor Fagotti.

SIMON BOCCANEGRA
VENICE, *March* 12th, 1857

Maria	Signora Bendázzi.
Gabriele	Signor Negrini.
Simon Boccanegra . .	Signor Giraldoni.
Paolo	Signor Vercellini.
Fiesco	Signor Eduverria.

[*Revised Version*]
MILAN, *March* 24th, 1881

Maria	Signora D'Angeri.
Gabriele	Signor Tamagno.
Simon Boccanegra . .	M. Maurel.
Paolo	Signor Salvati.
Fiesco	M. Edouard de Reszké.

ITALIAN MUSICAL COMPOSERS

AROLDO

RIMINI, *August 16th*, 1857

Mina	Signora Lotti.
Aroldo	Signor Pancani.
Godvino	Signor Poggiali.
Egberto	Signor Ferri.

UN BALLO IN MASCHERA

ROME, *February 17th*, 1859

Amelia	Madame Julienne-Dejean.
Edgar	Signora Scotti.
Ulrica	Signora Sbriscia.
Riccardo	Signor Fraschini.
Renato	Signor Giraldoni.

LONDON, *June 15th*, 1861

Amelia	Mdlle. Tietjens.
Edgar	Madame Gassier.
Ulrica	Madame Lemaire.
Riccardo	Signor Giuglini.
Renato	Signor Delle Sedie.

LA FORZA DEL DESTINO

ST. PETERSBURG, *November 10th*, 1862

Leonora	Madame Barbot,
Preziosilla	Madame Nantier-Didiée.
Alvaro	M. Tamberlik.
Carlo	Signor Graziani.

GIUSEPPE VERDI

LONDON, *June 22nd,* 1867

Leonora	Mdlle. Tietjens.
Preziosilla . . .	Madame Trebelli.
Alvaro	Signor Mongini.
Carlo	Mr. Santley.

DON CARLOS

PARIS, *March 11th,* 1867

Elisabeth . . .	Madame Sass.
Eboli	Madame Gueymard.
Carlos	M. Morère.
Rodrigue	M. Faure.
Philip II. . . .	M. Obin.

LONDON, *June 4th,* 1867

Elisabeth . .	Mdlle. Pauline Lucca.
Eboli	Mdlle. Fricci.
Carlos	M. Naudin.
Rodrigue	Signor Graziani.
Philip II. . . .	M. Petit.

AIDA

CAIRO, *December 24th,* 1871

Aida	Signora Pozzoni.
Amneris	Signora Grossi.
Rhadames . . .	Signor Mongini.
Amonasro . . .	Signor Steller.
Ramfis	Signor Medini.
Il Re	Signor Costa.

ITALIAN MUSICAL COMPOSERS

LONDON, *June 22nd,* 1876

Aida	Madame Patti.
Amneris. . . .	Mdlle. Gindele.
Rhadames . . .	Signor Nicolini.
Amonasro . . .	Signor Graziani.
Ramfis	Signor Capponi.
Il Re	M. Feitlinger.

OTELLO

MILAN, *February 5th,* 1887

Desdemona . . .	Signora Pantaleoni.
Emilia	Madame Petrovich.
Otello	Signor Tamagno.
Iago	M. Maurel.
Cassio	Signor Paroli.

LONDON, *July 5th,* 1889

Desdemona . . .	Signora Cataneo.
Emilia	Signora Mattiuzzi.
Otello	Signor Tamagno.
Iago	M. Maurel.
Cassio	Signor Paroli.

FALSTAFF

MILAN, *February 9th,* 1893

Mistress Ford . . .	Signora Zilli.
Mistress Page . . .	Signora Guerrini.
Nannetta. . . .	Madame Stehle.
Mistress Quickly . .	Signora Pasqua.

GIUSEPPE VERDI

FALSTAFF (MILAN)—*continued.*

Fenton	M. Garbin.
Ford . . .	Signor Pini-Corsi.
Dr. Caius . . .	Signor Paroli.
Bardolfo	Signor Pelagalli-Rossetti.
Pistola	Signor Arimondi.
Sir John Falstaff . .	M. Maurel.

LONDON, *May* 19th, 1894

Mistress Ford . . .	Signora Zilli.
Mistress Page . . .	Signorina Kitzu.
Nannetta . .	Signora Olghina.
Mistress Quickly . .	Signorina Ravogli
Fenton	Signor Beduschi.
Ford	Signor Pini-Corsi.
Dr. Caius . . .	Signor Armandi.
Bardolfo	Signor Pelagalli-Rossetti.
Pistola	Signor Arimondi.
Sir John Falstaff . .	Signor Pessina.

MISCELLANEOUS WORKS

SIX ROMANCES

Non t'accostare all' urna.
More, Elisa, lo stanco poeta.
In solitaria stanza.
Nell' orror di notte oscura.
Perduta ho la pace.
Deh ! pietoso.

135

ITALIAN MUSICAL COMPOSERS

L Esule . . .	Song for a Bass voice.
La Seduzione . .	Song for a Bass voice.
Guarda la bianca luna	Nocturne for three voices.

SIX ROMANCES

Il Tramonto.
La Zingara.
Ad una stella.
Lo Spazzacamino.
Il Mistero.
Brindisi.

Il Poveretto	Romanza.
Tu dici che non m'ami . . .	Stornello.

Inno delle Nazioni. 1862.
Messa da Requiem. 1874.
Pater Noster. Five-part chorus. 1880.
Ave Maria. Soprano solo, with string accompaniment. 1880.

String Quartet in E minor. 1873.

Arrigo Boito
3. Ottobre 94.
Milano

ARRIGO BOITO

ALTHOUGH Arrigo Boito's musical baggage is of the lightest, he bears a name which stands high among the masters of contemporary Italian music, and the honorary degree which was accorded to him in 1893 by the University of Cambridge testifies to the admiration which his genius has excited in this country. Boito presents the curious spectacle of a composer apparently without ambition. He is a musical edition of the famous "one-speech" Hamilton. After winning universal and sustained success with his first work, he has been content to remain a spectator for the rest of his life, and even to assist at other men's triumphs. The truth is that Boito is really more

137

of a poet than a musician, and important as was
the production of " Mefistofele " to the history
of Italian music, I doubt whether his influence
has not been more deeply felt in the admirable
libretti which from time to time he has written
for his friends. Without him the development of Verdi's genius would never have
reached its latest and crowning phase. The
music of " Otello " and " Falstaff " could not
have been written to the hack verses of a
mediocre librettist. In this case the poet and
musician have marched hand in hand, and in
the new era of Italian music heralded by these
two masterpieces Boito's name will be honoured
side by side with that of Verdi himself.

Arrigo Boito was born in Padua in 1842.
His father was an artist of considerable reputation. His mother was a Pole, the Countess
Josephine Radolinski. Those who are learned
in the doctrines of heredity may possibly
find the traces of Boito's mixed parentage
in his music, in the equal sympathy with
which he treats the dreamy mysticism of the

138

North and the sensuous passion of the South, but it is more profitable to note that the first influences with which he was brought into contact were calculated to foster a sense of beauty. His father's artistic gifts appeared more decisively in Camillo, his elder brother, a man of much originality and power, who is now Professor of Architecture at the Brera in Milan, and is a well-known and highly esteemed writer upon art. Camillo's influence upon his younger brother must have been important and decisive. As a boy Arrigo manifested no conspicuous talent for music, but by the time he reached the age of fourteen the general bent of his inclination was so obvious that the family moved to Milan, in order to enable him to attend the classes of the *Conservatorio*. Here he made the acquaintance of the men who were to exercise the most powerful influence over his future, Emilio Praga, the Baudelaire of Italy, a poet of uncommon genius, Alberto Mazzucato, under whom he studied at the *Conservatorio*, and many others.

In Milan, Boito was plunged into the full tide of Italian musical life. But even in Milan, which then as now was the musical capital of Italy, music meant nothing but opera. German music was practically unknown south of the Alps, and Boito's opportunities of becoming acquainted with the masterpieces of instrumental composers must have been very few and far between. Fortunately for him, Mazzucato was a man of singularly wide and enlightened sympathies. He soon discerned the promise of his pupil, and it was solely through his influence that Boito was enabled to complete his course of study, for at one time the authorities at the *Conservatorio* were so dissatisfied with his progress that they made up their minds to dismiss him. Curious as this may seem in the light of Boito's subsequent success, we must not forget that their predecessors were as little able to appreciate the latent genius of Verdi, while even Wagner's early years gave little promise of what he was ultimately to become. Throughout his

life, Boito's sympathies have been almost
equally divided between literature and music,
and it is extremely probable that at this time
the facilities for reading which the Brera
Library gave him rather hindered than advanced the progress of his musical studies.
No one, however, would suggest that this
enlargement of his literary horizon could have
other than a happy effect upon his music,
while his *libretti*, which are so strikingly remote
from clap-trap and provincialism, could only
have been written by a man of the widest
culture. As a matter of fact, it was as a
writer that he first attracted public notice.
Articles which he contributed to various French
and Italian magazines were highly praised, and
even attracted the favourable notice of Victor
Hugo. But his first real triumph was a
musical one. It took the shape of a cantata—
" Le Sorelle d'Italia "—of which Boito wrote
the *libretto* and part of the music, the rest being
provided by his fellow-pupil, Franco Faccio.
The score of this cantata has unfortunately

been lost, but records of its performance remain, and from all accounts it must have been a really remarkable work. A tangible proof of this was given by the Italian Government, which rewarded the two young composers with a sum of money to enable them to travel for two years in Europe, and study the works of foreign musicians.

Faccio's career came to an untimely end a few years ago, but he lived long enough to create a reputation as the finest living Italian conductor and the composer of " Amleto," an opera of much originality and beauty, the *libretto* of which was written by his friend Boito. He visited England in 1889, and acted as conductor during the short season at the Lyceum Theatre, which introduced "Otello" to a London audience for the first time.

Boito's European tour seems hardly to have had that effect upon him which the Italian Government contemplated. Meyerbeer he had known and admired before, so that the per-

formance of his works in Paris did not by any
means open up new worlds before him ; but it
seems singular that Wagner's operas, which he
certainly heard in Germany, should have made
so little impression upon him. It is impossible
to believe that Boito could have listened
unmoved to the beauties of " Lohengrin," but at
a first hearing he may have failed to grasp the
" true inwardness " of its subject, so unlike that
of any Italian opera, and so differently treated.
At any rate, he returned to Milan with his old
ideals undisturbed. He still found that Marcello, Beethoven, Verdi, and Meyerbeer spoke
the language which he understood best, and
indeed in his choice of divinities he was far
in advance of the existing standard of Italian
musical taste. Boito's career certainly never
ran in the ordinary groove. The Milanese
connoisseurs might reasonably have expected to
find the experiences and impressions of his two
years' travel embodied in some musical form,
but if so, they were doomed to disappointment.
After his return Boito devoted hi energies

almost exclusively to literature and journalism. His " Mefistofele," it is true, he had always more or less in hand, and a good deal of it dates from even earlier than this period. But the success of Gounod's " Faust " probably dispelled any notion he may have entertained of producing a work on the same story. Moreover, his theories were in rather a chaotic state, and it is doubtful if at this time he had really made up his mind as to what was the proper musical vehicle for his ideas. At this time he was an active contributor to the *Giornale della Società del Quartetto di Milano*, a newspaper which had lately been started, principally through the influence of his old professor Mazzucato, with the hope of doing something to reform the musical taste of Milan. This, too, is the period when most of his " Libro dei Versi " was written, though it was not published until ten years afterwards ; and his one novel, " L'Alfier Meno," also dates from the same epoch.

Boito has always been famous for the catholicity of his sympathies, and his ardent championship of Mendelssohn in the pages of the *Giornale* came near to bringing him into serious difficulties. A duel was the result, in which the youthful hero got wounded, and went about for some time with his arm in a sling. It seems as if time had not by any means tamed Boito's ardour, for little more than a year ago there were rumours of his being again upon the war-path, this time on behalf of an English composer. Fortunately, however, on this occasion matters did not come to a crisis. The earlier adventure sounds rather ridiculous to English ears, but it proves to what a length Protection in matters musical was carried in Milan, and how fierce an opposition the Free-traders had to contend against. Even now Italy is the most stubbornly conservative country, musically speaking, in Europe, though the improvement in the standard of taste since the sixties is of course enormous. 1866 was a stirring time in Milan, and in the excitement of the war with Austria music and journalism were both thrust into the background. So good a patriot as Boito was of course among the volunteers, and, together with Praga, Faccio, and other friends, he enlisted under Garibaldi. Poets and musicians are not as a rule very famous warriors, but Boito came out of the ordeal more successfully than his countryman Horace. There is no story of a "relicta non bene parmula." On the contrary, several of the musical recruits received special compliments upon their bravery.

When the war was over, Boito felt disinclined to go back to the drudgery of Milanese journalism, and decided to make a fresh start in Paris. He had letters of introduction to some of the leading Parisian journalists, and if all had gone smoothly he would probably have been lost to music altogether. But, luckily for us, Émile de Girardin, to whom he was specially recommended, was either unable or unwilling to help him, and after lingering for some time in Paris, Boito gave up his scheme in despair, and set off to visit his sister in Poland.

He probably felt bitterly disappointed at his

failure to take Paris by storm, but the check
which he had experienced threw him once more
into the arms of music. The peaceful life in
a Polish country house was an incentive to
work, and under these favouring conditions his
" Mefistofele " began to assume a definite shape.
But in spite of a renewed interest in his *magnum
opus*, he had already made up his mind to return
to Paris, when an event happened which—if
such things exist—was to prove the turning-
point of his career. Theatrical managers are
proverbially omniscient, and somehow or other
Signori Bonola and Brunello had got wind of
" Mefistofele." While Boito was still in Poland,
came the offer to produce his work at La Scala
during the season of 1867-68. There is something rather mysterious about this part of Boito's
history. Why should the *impresari* of an important theatre go out of their way to secure
the work of a young and absolutely inex-
perienced composer? His musical reputation
rested entirely upon the cantata " Le Sorelle
d'Italia," which had never been published

and only once performed. He was known no
doubt as a brilliant writer and a man of advanced
ideas, but it seems almost certain that the
Milanese connoisseurs of that day must have had
opportunities of gauging his musical capabilities
of which we know nothing.

All the preliminaries were soon arranged,
and " Mefistofele " was announced side by side
with Gounod's " Roméo et Juliette " and Verdi's
" Don Carlos " as one of the three operas which
every manager who takes the Teatro alla Scala
is bound to produce.

It is hardly necessary to say that "Mefistofele"
in its original condition was very different to
Boito's opera as we now know it. Before its
production at Bologna in 1875 the composer
subjected it to the most rigorous curtailment
and revision. It is a matter of regret that the
original score has never been published. It
would be extremely interesting to compare the
two versions, but as this is denied us we can
only fall back upon the descriptions of the first
night furnished by those who were present.

From all accounts it must have been a "record" even for Milan, where stormy *premières* are anything but a rarity. Public feeling had been worked up to a great pitch of excitement, and for weeks the new opera had been the talk of the town. Boito was already a well-known figure in Milan, and the advanced party both in music and literature looked upon him as one of their most promising adherents. From what had leaked out during the rehearsals as to the originality and beauty of the music it seemed that "Mefistofele" was to be the Hernani of a new era in Italian music. The fact that both *libretto* and music were from the pen of Boito seemed to presage the advent of an Italian Wagner. Several days before the production of the opera all the reserved seats were sold, although the prices had been raised to a height which at that time was unprecedented. Those who could not get seats took all the neighbouring *cafés* by storm, so as to get the first intelligence of the fate of the opera.

The rule of the theatre, which forbids a composer to conduct his own work was set aside for this occasion, and Boito had the doubtful privilege of conducting his " Mefistofele " in person.

His reception was enthusiastic, and after the Prologue, which was for the most part the same as that which is now performed, the applause was general. But after this everything went wrong. The succeeding scenes were immensely long—they have since been shortened and some of them cut out altogether—and the audience became impatient. Those who knew Gounod's " Faust " compared it with " Mefistofele " much to the latter's disadvantage, while those who did not, soon lost the thread of the story altogether. The lack of Bellinesque tune was fatal, and by the end of the second act it was evident that " Mefistofele " was not to be a success.

Boito's friends stood by him manfully, but their enthusiasm only aggravated the displeasure of the others, and after a performance lasting six hours the opera ended in a free fight. The enraged audience invaded the orchestra, and

literally hunted Boito out of the theatre. The
night that was to have marked an epoch in
Italian Music ended in shame and disgrace.
For once the public seems to have been right.
Boito's wholesale reconstruction of his work is
an admission of the justice of the Milanese
verdict. The fact is, that it was finished and
mounted in too great a hurry. The orchestration
was very weak, and the book was prolix and
incoherent to the last degree. Some writers
have gone so far as to speak of the earlier version
of "Mefistofele" as the true expression of
Boito's poetic and musical theories, and the
latter as a mere acting edition prepared for
every-day audiences because of the hardness of
their hearts. But Boito is scarcely the man to
have bent before the gusts of popular prejudice
so far as to mutilate his darling work to please
the fancy of the groundlings. He probably
recognised the justice of many of the hard
sayings which were showered upon him after
that unlucky *début* at La Scala, and in the
Bolognese version of "Mefistofele" we have his

original idea cleansed and purified by seven
years of searching analysis and self-criticism.
But the circumstances which attended its
reproduction were altogether more favourable
than before. In Bologna, the Bayreuth of Italy
as it has been named, the musical atmosphere
was not so stiflingly conservative as at Milan,
though even in the Lombard capital the lapse of
seven years had lessened the prejudice against
anything novel which had been so fatal to the
earlier version of " Mefistofele." The cast, too,
which included Signori Campanini, Nannetti,
and Signora Borghi-Mamo, was exceptionally
good. Boito had made several concessions to
popular taste. Faust was changed from a
baritone to a tenor, and provided with two tune-
ful romances, while the graceful Serenata was also
a complete novelty. But the most important
changes were in the Brocken scene and in the
opening of the first act. An immense amount
was cut out, and both scenes reduced to more
normal dimensions. One scene, too, later in
the opera, describing the battle between the

Emperor and pseudo-Emperor, was omitted
altogether. The orchestration was entirely remodelled, and from being the weakest became
one of the strongest points of the opera.
"Mefistofele" as we now have it gives us in
brief a picture of the gradual development of
the composer's genius. The success of its
reproduction at Bologna was decisive, and
quickly spread to other Italian cities. In
England it was not heard until 1880, when Mr.
Mapleson produced it at Her Majesty's Theatre
with Madame Christine Nilsson in the dual *rôle*
of Margaret and Helen. Its success here was
very great, and Madame Nilsson's rendering of
the character of Margaret was on the whole the
finest performance of her career. Since her
retirement from the stage Boito's opera has
been heard less and less often, and there seems
a danger of its dropping out of the current
European *répertoire* altogether.

Regrettable as this is, it is not difficult to
explain. Boito's *libretto* is a noble poem, and
reproduces the spirit of Goethe with singular

felicity, but from the merely scenic point of view it has many weaknesses. The principal failing is the lack of one thread of interest. The opera is merely a succession of episodes, each nicely calculated to throw a fresh light upon the character of Faust, but by no means mutually connected. Now, if there is one thing more essential than another to the permanent success of an opera, it is a lucid and simple story. No amount of subtle characterisation can make up for the lack of this. Gounod's French librettists knew their business thoroughly, and with characteristic *savoir-faire* fastened on the episode of Margaret, and threw overboard all the rest. Boito, in attempting to put a condensed version of the entire poem on the stage, gets hopelessly befogged in the mazes of Goethe's didactic allegory, and the individual beauty of many of the scenes is not enough to rivet the attention of an ordinary opera-goer.

Symbolism has lately invaded the dramatic stage, but with scant success. On the operatic stage it is even less in place. It is useless to

tell audiences that the episode of Helen and
the Classical Sabbath is an allegorical presentment of the union of the classical and romantic
ideals. They see nothing in it but a very
volatile hero consoling himself with a new love
for the loss of the old with almost indecent
promptitude, while the last scene, the salvation of
Faust, seems a violation of poetical justice, and
there is a generally expressed dissatisfaction that
Margaret's seducer is not carried off by Mephistopheles down the conventional trap-door.

But though Boito's devotion to Goethe has
militated against the permanent success of his
opera as a whole, the extraordinary beauty of
several single scenes ought surely to secure such
immortality for " Mefistofele " as the operatic
stage has to offer. The Prologue in Heaven is
scenically impossible, and in spite of the massive
grandeur of the choral writing it can hardly be
pronounced an effective realisation of Goethe's
idea. The opening of the first act, with its
piquant " Obertas," is very fresh and delightful,
but in the scene of the compact between

Mephistopheles and Faust the composer seems
to me hardly to have risen to the dignity of the
situation. Margaret is his happiest inspiration,
and the two scenes in which she appears are
masterpieces of beauty and pathos. In the
Garden Scene he has caught the ineffable simplicity of her character with astonishing success.
The contrast between her girlish purity and
the voluptuous sentiment of Gounod's heroine
cannot fail to be patent to the most careless
listener. The climax to this scene, the delightfully tender and playful quartet culminating
in a burst of hysterical laughter, is as profoundly true as it is dramatically impossible.
The artists who can sing such "catchy" music
while playing hide-and-seek behind the bushes
of the garden have yet to be found. Generally
the singers stand placidly in front of the footlights with their eyes glued to the conductor's
stick, a proceeding which hardly realises the
composer's intentions. The Witches' Sabbath is
a *tour de force*, and is besides wonderfully effective when properly staged, but the following

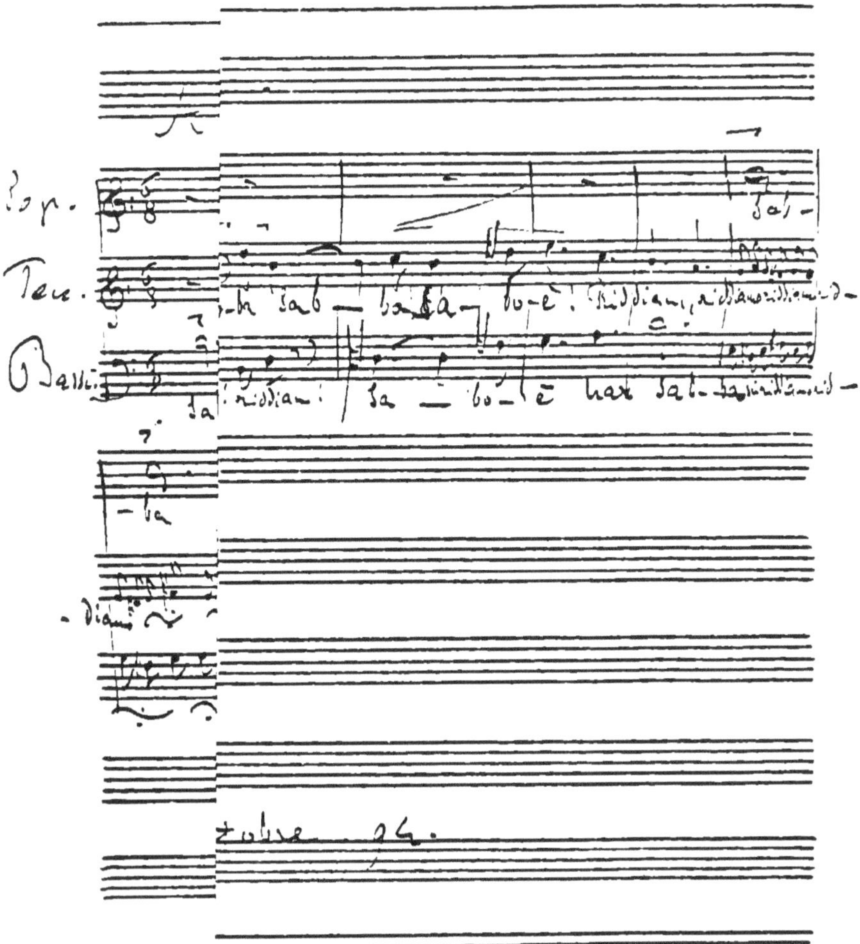

Sopr.
Ten.
Bassi

FACSIMILE OF AUTOGRAPH SCORE BY BOITO
"Mefistofele," Act II., Fuga Infernale

scene — the death of Margaret — is Boito's masterpiece. The poignant pathos of the poor maniac's broken utterances, the languorous beauty of the duet, and the frenzied terror and agony of the *Finale* are beyond praise. I must be pardoned for dwelling upon one exquisite point in the "Nenia" with which the scene opens, because I once saw a criticism in which it was urged that Boito had injured the effect of this beautiful song by introducing a commonplace *cadenza* at the close. Margaret sings :

> " La mesta anima mia
> Come il passero del bosco
> Vola via."

At the word "vola" her voice wanders up and down the scale of E minor, alighting at the close upon an F sharp *pianissimo*, while her thoughts wander back to happier days. But the terrible present suddenly breaks upon her. A crashing minor chord dispels her tender memories. She gasps out, "Ah, di me pietà," and falls swooning to the ground. Could anything be more subtly conceived ?

In the scene of the Classical Sabbath Boito set himself the task of musically interpreting Goethe's allegory of the union of Classicism and Romanticism. Consequently in the opening of the scene he made Helen and her attendants speak in unrhymed dactylic and choriambic verse (for Faust has not yet taught them his " idioma soave "), and wrote the accompanying music with an intentional disregard of modern rules of harmony. After the production of " Mefistofele " the consecutive fifths in the introductory symphony were severely criticised by pedants, but Boito's idea appears to me to be an excellent one in itself, and carried out with a fine sense of artistic truth. The concerted piece with which the act ends, in which is depicted the embrace of the Greek and Germanic ideals, has sensuous beauty enough to recommend it to any critic. The closing scene of the opera is certainly something of an anti-climax, musically speaking, though the return of the theme of the Prologue makes a majestic choral *Finale*.

Boito is perhaps of all living musicians the

most difficult to discuss fairly. No one who
has written so little has had so widely extended
an influence. In England we have not known
much until the last two or three years of contemporary Italian music. But all that has
reached us has testified most strongly to the
overmastering nature of Boito's influence. The
mere mention of " La Gioconda " is enough to
prove this. The most superficial hearer of
Ponchielli's masterpiece could not fail to be
struck by the close resemblance that exists
between the methods of the two composers.
Through Ponchielli, too, Boito has influenced
and is still influencing what, for the sake of
brevity, we call the school of " Young Italy " in
a very remarkable manner. But this influence
is easily accounted for when we think how very
much in advance of its age " Mefistofele " was,
and how strongly opposed to the lyric conven-
tions of 1868.

With " Aida " as yet unwritten, Verdi's genius
was still, so to speak, in the chrysalis stage.
Consequently, the truth and vigour of Boito's

declamation, and his freedom from the conventionality which was then all-powerful in Italy, seemed all the more remarkable, and made "Mefistofele," even in its fall, a kind of rallying point for the disciples of realism and nature in music.

Why "Mefistofele" has never had a successor is a difficult point to settle. Boito is really a poet by nature, and perhaps we ought to look upon his sole excursion into the domain of music as the brilliant feat of an amateur rather than the first step of a professional career. It is not difficult to find a parallel to such a case, at any rate in literature. Beckford's "Vathek"—though Dr. Garnett's recent discoveries forbid us to speak of it any longer as the work of a single sitting—has perhaps something of its fantastic beauty, something too of its unreality and symbolism. Certainly the two works, apart from the curiously isolated position which they occupy in their respective spheres, are equally remarkable for their glowing colour and imaginative power. The supposition that Boito has said all his say

in " Mefistofele," that he has put forward all his
theories upon the lyric drama crystallised into
one opera, is scarcely tenable. Boito's views on
his art are too well known to allow us to suppose
him incapable of progress beyond a fixed point,
and that point his own twenty-year-old opera.
Indeed not long ago he spoke of " Mefistofele "
to a Parisian interviewer with rather more than
his habitual modesty as " un vieux rossignol."
From time to time the world has been entertained with the rumours of a finished " Nerone."
A few favoured mortals have been permitted to
hear occasional extracts from it in the dreadful
secrecy of the composer's study. But whether
it is ever to see the footlights is a question
between Boito and his conscience.

If the long-promised work is ever actually
performed—and it must be ten years since it was
announced as completed—we may expect in it to
find Boito fully abreast of the latest development
of opera. But musicians have almost given up
hope of a successor to " Mefistofele." The fact
is, that Boito is really too acute a critic to be a

composer. He knows so well what good music is, that he mistrusts his own powers. He is so determined that we shall have nothing from him but the very best that we end by getting nothing at all, and I fear that on the whole we must part from him with the words which were written of another poet, Thomas Gray, whose fastidious self-criticism so fatally stunted his productive power—" He never spoke out."

PIETRO MASCAGNI

MUSICIANS sometimes complain of the dis-
advantages under which they labour as compared
with painters. A picture, they say, hangs upon
the wall, and connoisseurs may study it at their
leisure ; they may examine it from this point
and that, from near and from far, until beauties
at first unperceived gradually reveal themselves,
and at last the painter's inmost thought stands
manifest to the light of day. But a musical
composition, they say, is heard once and for all.
It passes and is gone, and can leave nothing but
a general impression in the mind of the hearer.
This is certainly true, and much noble music
has suffered thereby, but for this very reason it
is only in music that those sudden and instan-

taneous triumphs are possible, which occasionally surprise the world. When a prolonged scrutiny is out of the question, if the salient features of a work are striking and original, faults of detail are either forgotten or forgiven.

Those who have witnessed the fevered raptures of an Italian *première* know something of the compensations which Music grants to her votaries. What is the decorous admiration of a private view to the tempestuous triumph which occasionally falls to the lot of some fortunate *maestro?* What does it matter to him if he wakes up the next morning to find his opera torn to shreds by captious critics, or to hear that his *impresario* has decamped with the cashbox?

One naturally thinks of Italy in connection with musical enthusiasm, for on that arden soil boisterous successes are by no means rare. In the cold North, it is true, we have come to regard these periodical ebullitions with suspicion. The laurels of the South wither in the keener climate of our inhospitable shores. During

the last few years, however, Italy has been
justified of her raptures in a very remarkable
manner. The extraordinary success of "Cavalleria Rusticana" is still fresh in our memories.
Before the production of his little opera Pietro
Mascagni was not merely obscure, he was absolutely unknown. He is now one of the most
famous of living composers. "Cavalleria Rusticana" has been performed upon almost every
operatic stage in the world, and everywhere
with the same success. Even where critics
came to sneer, the public remained to applaud.
Whatever may be Mascagni's ultimate fate, it
cannot be denied that his first work scored one
of the most genuine triumphs in the history of
music.

Pietro Mascagni was born at Leghorn on
December 7th, 1863. His father, Domenico,
was a baker, but though his origin was not
exactly illustrious nor his environment artistic,
the young composer was evidently not born to
poverty, for his father seems early to have made
up his mind to make him a lawyer. With that

laudable object in view, he was sent to school. Everything went well at first ; Pietro was industrious and earned golden opinions from his teachers. But before long his studies took a different direction. He struck up a friendship with a certain Signor Bianchi, a teacher of singing, who must be complimented on being the first to discover the boy's talent for music. His father heard with some annoyance of this new departure, but bore it—singing-lessons and all—with resignation, until he discovered attempts at composition scattered about his son's room. This was no laughing matter, and he proceeded to exercise summary judgment by cramming them one and all into the fire. His anger, however, was short-lived, and he made noble amends by presenting his son with an old piano, picked up second-hand. Yet even now he did not realise the boy's real vocation, and still adhered to his plan of making him a lawyer. Pietro, however, took the matter into his own hands, and surreptitiously entered himself as a pupil at the Istituto Luigi Cherubini.

There he was placed under Signor Alfredo
Soffredini, and began to find out something of
what music really was. His studies then pur-
sued the even tenor of their way for some time,
but when Domenico found out what had been
going on, he was very angry indeed. Nothing
would do but that the music should be given up
once and for all. In vain Soffredini pleaded and
promised that Pietro would bring eternal glory
to the name of Mascagni. Domenico was obdu-
rate. Luckily a *deus ex machinâ* appeared in
the shape of Pietro's uncle, Stefano. He nobly
came forward and offered to adopt his young
nephew. This was agreed to, and Pietro went
to live with his uncle, who proceeded to seal
the bargain with the purchase of a new piano, a
veritable godsend to the budding composer. In
his uncle's house the time passed pleasantly.
Soffredini's lessons and the new piano soon bore
fruit in the shape of a Symphony in C minor
for small orchestra, and a " Kyrie " written in
celebration of the birthday of Cherubini. These
were both performed at the Istituto in 1879.

Two years later followed a work of wider scope,
"In Filanda," a cantata for solo voices and
orchestra. A shadow was cast over Mascagni's
life at this time by the death of the uncle who
had been so truly his friend. Stefano lived
long enough to see "In Filanda" favourably
mentioned at the International Exhibition of
Music at Milan, but he could scarcely have
had any suspicion of the extraordinary success which the future had in store for his
nephew.

After his uncle's death Mascagni returned to
the paternal roof. Time had worked wonders,
and his father was now completely reconciled to
the idea of a musical career. Pietro was allowed
to pursue his studies in peace. His next effort
was a setting of Schiller's Ode "An die Freude,"
which was performed at the Teatro Avvalorati.
So great was its success and so evident was the
talent of the young composer that Count
Florestano de Larderel came forward on the
spot and offered to pay for his education at the
Milan Conservatoire. The offer was gratefully

accepted and Mascagni started forthwith for the musical capital of Italy.

His career in Milan was not a success. There are some men to whom the trivial round, the common task is an insupportable burden. Mascagni was one of these. His professors were sympathetic and encouraging. With Michele Saladino in particular he formed a close friendship, founded upon gratitude and admiration. His comrades were friendly and generous. To Puccini, another composer who has since become famous, he was united by bonds of the warmest intimacy. Nevertheless, he remained restless and unsettled. Like Schubert before him, he chafed under the rod of fugue and counterpoint. The success of Puccini's opera, "Le Villi," was the last straw. Not that there was any question of envy, for Mascagni was the first to rush on to the stage of the Teatro dal Verme to congratulate his friend ; but Puccini's triumph, like the victories of Miltiades which disturbed the slumbers of Themistocles, seemed to bid Mascagni go and do likewise. Like

Cleopatra, he had "immortal longings" in him.
He could bear the plodding life at Milan no
longer, and one day he disappeared suddenly.
No one knew whither he had gone. The
waves seemed to have closed over his head,
and after a time even his friends left off won-
dering what had become of him.

The tale of Mascagni's wanderings scarcely
needs a Homer. He joined a travelling operatic
troupe under the management of an *impresario*
named Forli, with which he visited Piacenza,
Reggio, and Parma. In the last-named city he
appeared for the first time as conductor, the
operetta performed being Lecocq's " Le Cœur
et la Main." In Bologna the company broke
up. This was in 1885. Mascagni was thrown
upon the world, but he determined to do anything rather than return disgraced and disappointed to Leghorn, which he left a few years
before with such lofty hopes. He soon joined
another travelling company, and for the next
few years he spent all his time wandering over
the face of Italy with one or another of these

troupes. It was a hand-to-mouth existence, and he often scarcely knew where to look for a meal; but the experiences which he gained of the various instruments in the orchestra proved invaluable, and gave him more practical know-ledge of orchestration than any amount of theo-rising could have done. Mascagni happened to find himself at Ascoli one fine day, when for the hundredth time the company with which he was travelling suddenly broke up. The composer had contrived to save a little money, and he deter-mined to stay quietly in the little Umbrian city and finish his opera " Guglielmo Ratcliff," which he had begun in his student days at Milan. In less than three weeks he finished the fourth act, and then found to his dismay that his savings were exhausted. There was nothing for it but to start again on his travels, with another of these interminable companies. But the hard-ships of this wandering life were too much for the young composer. He fell ill at Naples, and was only nursed back to life by the devotion of the young lady who afterwards became his wife. After their wedding the wandering life began again. They left Naples and visited Foggia, and afterwards made their way to Cerignola. Here Mascagni made friends among the good people of the town, and decided, "in deference to a generally expressed desire," to give up his travelling and settle down as a teacher of the pianoforte. But the pupils were few and far between, and the price of music lessons was very low, so that the composer and his wife were reduced to terrible straits. To give him a helping hand the municipality started an orchestral school, of which he was appointed director, and he soon managed to form a full orchestra. But this did not mend matters much, and Mascagni's bread and water were not sweetened by the thought that he had buried himself in this out-of-the-way little place far from all chance of distinction. Still, he did not give up hope, and worked away indefatigably, though the future before him seemed dark and unpromising. Suddenly the announcement of one of Signor Sonzogno's "Concorsi" caught his eye in a newspaper. The publisher offered handsome prizes for the three best one-act operas upon any subject, which were to be produced in Rome free of expense. Mascagni made up his mind at once to enter for the competition, and wrote off to two of his friends at Leghorn, Signori Targioni-Tozzetti and Menasci, for a *libretto*. They agreed to do their best, and started forthwith upon the poem of "Cavalleria Rusticana."

The time was short, and Mascagni could not wait until the *libretto* was finished; so the two authors sent him their work piecemeal, scene by scene—sometimes only a few lines upon the back of a post-card. Mascagni wrote with feverish haste, but only just contrived to finish and pack off his score before the "Concorso" closed. Then came a period of anxious wait- ing, while the jury deliberated upon the merits of the competitors. At last the result was declared. The first prize was adjudged to "Cavalleria Rusticana"; second and third came "Labilia," by Nicolo Spinelli, and

"Rudello," by Ferroni, one of the professors at the Milan Conservatoire. The result was announced early in March. Two months later came the first performance of the successful works. On the 20th of May 1890 "Labilia" and "Cavalleria Rusticana" were produced at the Costanzi Theatre in Rome. The famous singers, Gemma Bellincioni and Roberto Stagno, appeared in both works. The success of "Labilia" was only moderate, but "Cavalleria" roused the audience to a frenzy of enthusiasm. Mascagni was called twenty times before the curtain, and the next morning all the Roman newspapers declared that Verdi's successor had at length been discovered. The second and third performance of the opera took place with even increased success. By this time Mascagni had become famous. The town of Cerignola created him an honorary citizen; his native Leghorn struck a medal in his honour; the King of Italy made him Chevalier of the Order of the Crown of Italy, an honour not accorded to Verdi until he had reached middle-life. Meanwhile *impresari* fought for the new opera. Every theatre in Italy hastened to secure it, and translators at once set to work to turn out English, French, and German editions of the *libretto*. Mascagni's return to Leghorn was a kind of triumphal progress. The city was illuminated, the streets were crowded, bands played serenades under the composer's window. In a word, Italy lost her head over "Cavalleria." But even when the first wave of excitement had passed away, the popularity of the little opera remained as steady as ever.

The story of "Cavalleria" is taken from a Sicilian story of the same name by the well-known Giovanni Verga. It had previously been dramatised and successfully produced in various Italian towns. More recently it has become famous both in Europe and America through the talent of Signora Duse, whose performance of Santuzza is one of the most striking of her many fine impersonations. The story lends itself peculiarly well to operatic purposes. Turiddu, a village Adonis, is beloved by the fair Lola. He enlists as a soldier, and on his return from the wars finds that the fickle damsel has taken advantage of his absence to marry Alfio, a carter. He looks round him for fresh conquests, and his choice falls upon Santuzza, whom he seduces. This arouses all Lola's latent coquetry, and she soon contrives to win him back to her side. The deserted Santuzza appeals in vain to his love and pity. He repulses her roughly, and, half-mad with rage and jealousy, she tells the whole story to Alfio. Alfio challenges Turiddu to a mortal encounter, and kills him as the curtain falls. This is the sort of story which it is the fashion to describe as "palpitating with actuality," and, squalid as it is, it has the merit of life and movement and a simple directness which is essential in a *libretto*. As to the music, there have been many different opinions, and a good deal of ink has been spilt over them. But there is one point which no amount of adverse criticism can explain away, and that is the success of Mascagni's little opera. It has

FACSIMILE OF AUTOGRAPH SCORE BY MASCAGNI
"*Cavalleria Rusticana*," *Scene V*.

never failed anywhere. Even in Paris, where
the press greeted its advent with a paroxysm
of Chauvinistic fury, the public was not to
be dissuaded from going to listen to it, and
the hundredth performance took place about
eighteen months after its original production.
In the face of these facts it is a mistaken policy
to attempt, as some critics have done, to brush
the piece aside with a few contemptuous remarks.
"Cavalleria" has many faults, but it also has
not a few good points, which only the blindest
prejudice can affect to ignore. The music is
sometimes not original, sometimes commonplace, sometimes vulgar, sometimes even coarse.
All this I freely admit. Young musicians,
especially when writing in a hurry, are rather
apt to confuse memory with inspiration, and
no generous critic will go out of his way
to docket some of Mascagni's melodies with
their unmistakable genealogies. It is more to
the point to observe that the young composer
has a copious stream of melody of his own to
draw upon. It is often rather *banal*, especially

when he is doing his best to be impressive, as in the duet between Santuzza and Turiddu; but it is also very often exceedingly fresh and charming, as in the Siciliana, sung behind the curtain during the overture, and the opening chorus, a number which sparkles with life and sunlight. But, besides his undoubted gift of melody, Mascagni has a very good idea of declamation. This is particularly evident in Santuzza's opening phrases and in her so-called Romance, a piece which is full of character and resource. It is difficult to say anything complimentary about the Prayer, which is as commonplace as one of Gounod's worst *cantiques*, or the Brindisi, which is mere opera-bouffe. But there is a good deal of feeling and passion of the right sort in Turiddu's farewell, and the final scene of the opera is admirably managed. We are all sick of the Intermezzo, of course, but that is the organ-grinder's fault, not the composer's. Mascagni's idea was undoubtedly a good one. He wanted to show us that while this storm-in-a-teacup was going on in a little

out-of-the-way Sicilian village, the world — to use
Mr. Gilbert's phrase—was rolling on just as
usual. He wished to convey the impression of
largeness and repose, which should come rest-
fully upon the ear after the wild passion of the
scene before. Unluckily, he thought he could
do this by means of a passage for the violins in
unison with a harp and organ accompaniment.
I doubt if Verdi himself could have done it.
The opening of the Intermezzo is well conceived,
and fully realises the idea which Mascagni had
in his mind, but the second half is—well, it has
hit the popular taste. But, unequal as it is,
"Cavalleria Rusticana" contains so much that
is original, and so much that is full of promise
for the future, that it would be ungracious
to grudge it its overwhelming success. How
seldom has the first work of even one of the
greatest masters of music contained a tithe of
the promise—ay, and of the performance too—
of "Cavalleria Rusticana"!

Those who were wise made it known that
after the triumph of "Cavalleria Rusticana,"

they would give Mascagni some years to regain his normal musical temperature, and would not expect any serious work from him in the meantime. Youth is youth, and composers are but human.

The success of "Cavalleria" turned Mascagni's head. He thought that he had nothing more to do but to sit in an armchair for the rest of his life and scribble operas, which an appreciative world would at once swallow wholesale. He would have been a phenomenon if he had thought anything else. He is learning better now; but meanwhile I would protest most forcibly against the founding of a serious estimate of Mascagni's talents upon "L'Amico Fritz" and "I Rantzau." We must remember that, while a mere boy, he was taken from abject penury, and suddenly, one might almost say by a turn of the dice, raised to a position in which he not only had everything he could possibly want, but could command practically any price he liked for his music. It would obviously be unjust to take what he produced under these abnormal conditions as the natural product of his genius. In a few years he will sober down. "Cavalleria" will go the way of all ephemeral successes. Mascagni will find that he is not the only musician in the world, and then he will settle down to his career in good earnest. Meanwhile it is absurd to speak of him as a young man with an already extinct reputation, and so forth, merely because he does exactly what every sensible man knew from the first that he would do.

Every one was surprised to hear that Mascagni, who had made his name and fortune in double-dyed melodrama, had turned for his second *libretto* to an idyllic Alsatian story. Erck-mann-Chatrian's "L'Amico Fritz" was perhaps the most unpromising subject for an opera ever chosen by a musician. It is the more creditable to Signor Suardon that he contrived to extract from it a pretty little three-act *libretto*, which, though slight in fibre and woefully un-dramatic, is by no means uninteresting. One's first thought was that Mascagni was determined to show his versatility and astonish the world, after the very leonine raptures of " Cavalleria Rusticana," by appearing in the guise of a sucking dove. When " L'Amico Fritz " was produced at Rome, on the 31st October 1891, it turned out that it was nothing of the sort. Mascagni had tried to adapt the " Cavalleria " manner to his new *libretto*. He drove his village idyll home with a perfect pandemonium of trombones. Crashing cymbals accompanied an invitation to supper, banging drums announced its acceptance. The unfortunate story was drowned in oceans of orchestration. In the middle of all this noise and vulgarity came a duet so exquisitely fanciful and melodious, so full of all the charm of sunshine and springtime, as to make one wonder if it could possibly be the work of this genius of the storm. There was something terribly perverse about a man who could write like this descending to the extravagance and exaggeration which characterise so much of the opera.

This one number, the " Duetto delle Ciliege," was the saving of " L'Amico Fritz." For its

sake the sins of the rest of the score have been
partially condoned. For, to tell the truth, the
little opera is full of mannerisms of a pronounced
and unmistakable character. Not only, as I
have said, is the orchestration ridiculously
pompous and pretentious, but the composer
displays in it a love of tortured rhythms and
incessant changes of key which is positively
distracting. In any case, these tricks—for they
are nothing more—would be highly culpable,
but in a village story, where everything ought to
be especially simple and unpretending, they are
doubly objectionable. From every point of
view the opera was a mistake, for in spite of
his undeniable dramatic power Mascagni has
at present but little power of characterisation,
and his efforts to infuse local colour into his
music were very lame. It would indeed have
been a *tour de force* if an Italian composer of
Mascagni's age and experience had succeeded
in so far denationalising his genius as to absorb
the peculiarly local atmosphere of Erckmann-
Chatrian.

"L'Amico Fritz" ought to have satisfied Mascagni as to the present scope of his abilities. It did nothing of the sort. With a curious blindness to the real bent of his genius, he still clung to Erckmann-Chatrian and his Alsatian stories. "I Rantzau," his next work, which was performed for the first time at the Pergola Theatre in Florence on the 10th of November 1892, had little of the charm of "L'Amico Fritz," while in it the irritating mannerisms of its predecessor were still more strongly marked. The *libretto*, to begin with, by Signori Menasci and Targioni-Tozzetti, the authors of "Cavalleria Rusticana," was a singularly awkward piece of work.

A village "Romeo and Juliet," in which the hero and heroine do not meet until the fourth act, does not offer very promising material for a composer to work upon. But the *libretto* throughout is worse than clumsy; it is dull. The brothers Giacomo and Gianni, with their foolish feud, the tender-hearted old school-master, and even the lovers themselves, are

eminently uninteresting, and no amount of
orchestration, however volcanic, can galvanise
them into life. Mascagni's music is scarcely
more satisfactory than the *libretto*. As usual, he
has plenty of ideas, but they are in an amor-
phous and chaotic state, and he does not seem to
know what to do with them. All the defects of
" L'Amico Fritz" appear in " I Rantzau " in an
exaggerated form. The pretentious and mean-
ingless orchestration, the harsh and incessant
modulation and the vagueness of rhythm, are
even more pronounced than in the earlier work.
What can be said for a prelude of about a
hundred bars in which the time-signature is
changed no less than twenty-four times, or for a
village auction celebrated by a *Finale*, on the
pattern of " Aida," with rolling drums and blaring
trombones, while the principals stand in a semi-
circle by the footlights and the chorus bellows
behind? There is one charming number in " I
Rantzau "—the "Cicaleccio" a chorus of village
girls gossiping round a well—which is worthy
of Rossini in its grace and delicate finish. But

one swallow does not make a summer, and as a whole "I Rantzau" will not often be heard of again. Mascagni, if he is wise, will be the first to wish it buried in forgetfulness.

Since "Cavalleria," then, the young composer's career has been anything but a march from strength to strength. It is true that in "L'Amico Fritz" there are passages which show a degree of refinement which it would be vain to look for in the earlier work. But, speaking in general terms, there is no quality present in either of Mascagni's later works which we do not find more favourably represented in "Cavalleria Rusticana," without the accretion of tricks and mannerisms which do so much to disfigure his two last operas. As I have said above, I do not attach much importance to this. I look upon "L'Amico Fritz" and "I Rantzau" as Mascagni's musical wild oats. In thinking of his future we shall do well to regard them as a *quantité négligeable*. It would be too much to expect a series of masterpieces from a man of Mascagni's age. There is enough in "Cavalleria Rusti-

cana" to give promise of really stable and
lasting work, when the ardours of youth have
been tempered by a dose of experience.

As it is, he already seems to be partly conscious of his errors. The failure of " I Rantzau " opened his eyes to the position of affairs.
His early opera, " Guglielmo Ratcliff," had been
accepted at the Imperial Opera at Berlin, but
he insisted upon having the score back again,
and has since subjected it to a very stringent
system of revision. This is a good sign, and
shows that the young composer is not ashamed
to be guided by good advice. It is always
dangerous to prophesy, especially in the case
of the career of so young a man as Mascagni.
When there is so little upon which to ground
conclusions, no one's opinion is worth very much,
but Mascagni's achievements at least warrant
the hope that he will live to make a name of
which Italy will have reason to be proud.

While this book was passing through the press
two new operas by Mascagni have been given to

the world. The first, a revised version of his early work, "Guglielmo Ratcliff," was produced at the Teatro alla Scala in Milan on the 16th of February 1895; the second, "Silvano" by name, saw the light at the same theatre on the 25th of March. Both operas were favourably received.

GIACOMO PUCCINI

THOSE who look with disfavour on what, for the
sake of convenience, we call the school of "Young
Italy," are sometimes inclined to dismiss its
members *en masse* as merely a band of strenuous
innovators, without training or traditions, whom
a momentary craving for melodrama has raised
into undue prominence. But though the "Young
Italians" are bound by one common wish—to
free their national art from the empty conven-
tions of the last generation, and to breathe a new
life into its withered carcase—they are setting
about its accomplishment in different ways.
For instance, the divergences between Mascagni
and Puccini are at least as striking as the
resemblances. The circumstances of their birth

189

and education were at any rate singularly unlike. Mascagni, as we have seen, with almost every possible disadvantage, fought his way to success with a perseverance which, whatever we may think of his music, we cannot but admire. Puccini, on the other hand, was born of a race of musicians who for many years had occupied positions more or less estimable in the city of Lucca. Thus the two most promising of the younger Italian composers exemplify very strikingly the two forms in which musical genius is manifested—the inherited or derivative, and the innate or spontaneous.

Sometimes the creative gift is the product of a long line of musical ancestors, all of whom have had in greater or less degree a taste or a talent for music, until at length the combined powers of the family have united to produce the perfect flower of a consummate genius. At another time, we find, in the most uncongenial environment and under the most unfavourable conditions, a genius which appears complete within itself, owing nothing to external influences. Surely there

must be something radically different in the
talents that are produced in such different ways.
If we examine them, do we not find that the
creations of natures so diversely moulded appeal
to totally different classes of hearers? Let us
take instances of our two types of genius, and
compare them. Johann Sebastian Bach is evidently the classical specimen of the first. The
family of Bach had from the first a wonderful
gift of music. Veit Bach, the baker of Wech-
mar, the founder of the clan, was a noted
performer upon the "Cythringen." His sons
and grandsons were all musicians. All held
positions more or less honourable as organists
or composers; but in his descendant, Johann
Sebastian, the various genealogical threads
were finally knit together. He seems to have
absorbed within his own person all the elements
dispersed among his ancestors. The isolated
qualities which had been the individual possession of his many predecessors united in him to
form the most perfect musical organism ever
known. Bach's great contemporary, Handel,

is a type of the second class. Nothing could well have been less congenial than the atmosphere into which he was born. His father, a well-to-do surgeon of Halle, disliked the very sound of music ; nor were any of his relations much better. Every step he took in the cultivation of his innate musical sense had to be fought for in the teeth of all his family.

Here are the two types of musical genius. And now as to their character : will the man who combines in himself the united musicianship of generations write the same kind of music as the man who has drawn his genius straight from Nature herself? Will the work of the one appeal to the same class of hearer as that of the other? We should undoubtedly expect the former to write music which would commend itself specially to the ear of a musician, while the latter would speak more directly to the popular ear. Is not this exactly the case? Bach is pre-eminently the musician's musician, while Handel all the world over is the darling of the people.

I do not suggest for a moment that Bach is lacking in inspiration or Handel in science, I only wish to point out that the general characteristics of each man's music are such as would naturally be expected from his origin and environment.

The same theory holds good in the case of Puccini and Mascagni. Puccini, sprung from a long line of musical ancestors, has written music which has delighted connoisseurs, but outside his own country has not yet achieved any great popular success. Mascagni, the son of a baker, after the production of a solitary one-act opera became at a bound the most popular composer in Europe. In their little way, Puccini and Mascagni are the Bach and Handel of the " Young Italy" of to-day. Their music bears the ineffaceable seal of their birth and parentage. To sum it up in a word, one writes music of the head, the other of the heart.

Giacomo Puccini's great-great-grandfather, who was also named Giacomo, was born in 1712. He filled the office of *Maestro di*

Cappella to the Republic of Lucca, and was a composer of some reputation. We are not accustomed to regard the Italian sacred music of this period with exaggerated respect, but nevertheless it must be admitted that his Requiem for eight voices, which was included in the Vienna Musical Exhibition of 1892, is a workmanlike production. Giacomo the elder is also known as the master of Guglielmi, one of the most prolific and popular composers of the eighteenth century, who is now almost as completely forgotten as his master. Antonio Puccini, the son of Giacomo, was born in 1747. He appears to have been less famous as a composer than as a theorist. One of his works —a Kyrie and Gloria for eight voices—was also included in the Vienna Exhibition. Domenico his son, born in 1771, wrote operas as well as church music. Visitors to Vienna had the opportunity of becoming acquainted with his "Quinto Fabio" and with a Motet for sixteen voices of his composition. Michele, the son of Domenico, who was born in 1813. seems to have been a worthy descendant of this line of musicians. His reputation was more than local, and he was famous throughout North Italy as a scientific musician. His music is entirely sacred, and is spoken of by contemporary writers with the utmost respect. His death, which occurred at Lucca in 1864, was looked upon as little short of a national calamity, and his funeral, at which the well-known composer Pacini conducted a Requiem, was a most imposing affair. He was represented at Vienna by some Canons for thirty-two voices and other works. His son Giacomo, the composer of " Manon Lescaut," second of the name and the fifth musician of his family, was born at Lucca in 1858. He was one of a family of six, all of whom were so devoted to music that one who knew them well in those early days has described their house as a gigantic musical box. Giacomo, however, was the genius of the family, and his studies began at a very early age. The death of his father when he was six years old does not seem to have interrupted them to any appreciable extent, for his great-uncle, Dr. Nicolao Cerù, in whose charge he was placed, gave him all the assistance at his command. But a time came when Lucca had taught him all that it knew, and his thoughts turned towards Milan. Fortunately, the name of Puccini was one to conjure with, and this, combined with his own evident genius, secured him a pension from the Queen of Italy sufficient to enable him to make a start at the Milan Conservatoire. The pension only lasted for one year, but when this had expired Dr. Cerù again proved a *deus ex machina*, and supplied the necessities of aspiring genius from his own purse. It is the custom, as I have already said, for the authorities of the Conservatoire to give a performance of a work by the most successful of their pupils at the close of the course of studies. Puccini's contribution was a Sinfonia-Capriccio for orchestra, which was given with genuine success.

At the Conservatoire Puccini had been a pupil of Amilcare Ponchielli, and it was at the latter's suggestion that he undertook the com-

GIACOMO PUCCINI

position of an opera entitled " Le Villi " to the
libretto of Fontana. Puccini wrote this in view
of the first of the " Concorsi " instituted by the
publisher Sonzogno. It failed to win the prize,
but according to the composer's own confession
the score was so execrably written as to be
almost unreadable. Those who have had the
task of deciphering Puccini's caligraphy will not
be surprised that the judges failed altogether to
appreciate the beauties of " Le Villi " through
such a medium. But, though rejected, " Le
Villi " was by no means relegated to the waste-
paper basket. Every musician who had heard
the composer play his opera was struck by its
originality and imaginative power, and, principally owing to the kind offices of Arrigo Boito,
matters were soon so satisfactorily arranged that
the work was accepted and produced at the
Teatro dal Verme on the 31st of May 1884.

In its original form " Le Villi " was in one act.
The success of its production was so great that
the score was immediately purchased by the
firm of Ricordi, under whose auspices it was

performed at La Scala on the 24th of January 1885. Previous to this event Puccini had thoroughly revised his work and expanded it into two acts. The symphonic portions of the opera, which are certainly the most original and characteristic, date almost entirely from this revival.

It is necessary in discussing " Le Villi " to remember that it was written a good many years before " Cavalleria Rusticana," not that there is any reason to suppose that either of the two works owes anything to the other, but because it is sometimes said that Mascagni's opera started the race of one-act "shriekers " under which we are still labouring. There were kings, however, before Agamemnon, and Puccini's work preceeded " Cavalleria " by about six years. As a matter of fact, if there was a founder to the " Young Italian " school, it was neither Puccini nor Mascagni, but the publisher Sonzogno. He was clever enough to see that the public was tired of the old three-decker operas, and accordingly set about launching a fleet of

torpedo-boats by means of his famous "Concorsi." After all, these endless questions as to
whether this or that opera was written first, and
how much one owes to the other, and which
is the copy and which the original, are the
merest waste of time. If a work is good, it will
survive whenever and wherever it was produced.
As Renan says, every schoolboy now has at his
finger-ends what Archimedes would have given
his life to know. Mozart died more than a
hundred years ago, and every musician since his
day has learnt his scores by heart; but how
many " Don Juans" have we had?

The subject of " Le Villi" is a strange one to
have taken the fancy of a southern composer.
It is founded upon one of those weird traditions
which seem essentially the property of Northern
races. Villi, or, in English, Wilis, are, according
to the most authentic records, the spirits of
affianced damsels whose lovers have proved
untrue. They rise from the earth at midnight
and assemble on the highway attired in all their
bridal finery. From midnight to dawn they

wheel their wild dances, and watch for their faithless lovers. If one of the latter happen to pass, he is beguiled into the magic circle, and, in the grasp of the relentless Wilis, is whirled round and round until he sinks expiring on the ground. Keightley, the great authority on everything supernatural, speaks of the superstition as being of Servian origin. It probably is Slavonic, but traces of it are found in many Teutonic and Scandinavian literatures. It has been used before now by librettists. Adam's ballet "Giselle" is founded upon the legend, as is also Loder's " Night-Dancers," though in both works there are considerable variations from the original form. In Puccini's opera the scene is laid in the Black Forest. The characters are three in number—Anna, her *fiancé* Robert, and her father Wilhelm Wulf. The first act opens with the betrothal of the lovers. After merry-making of various kinds and a short prayer, Robert departs for Mayence, whither he has to go in order to claim an inheritance. Six months elapse between the first and second acts.

Robert has fallen into the toils of an abandoned woman and is still at Mayence. Anna has died of a broken heart. The second act opens with a symphonic movement, "L'Abbandono," while on the stage we see the funeral of Anna enacted, save for a mournful chorus, in dumb show. This is followed by a purely orchestral movement, "La Tregenda," which serves as an accompaniment to the weird dance of the Wilis, who are on the watch for Robert. After an air for the father, Robert appears. He is tortured by remorse, and in a long and passionate scene pours forth his unavailing regrets. But the hour for repentance is past; Anna appears, followed by the attendant Wilis. The wretched man, in a kind of hypnotic trance, is drawn into their ghostly circle. They whirl him round in ever wilder and more fantastic dances until he drops lifeless upon the earth, and his persecutors disappear with a "Hosanna" of triumph.

The music of "Le Villi" is the work of a man of imagination. It is thoroughly Italian in character, and there is little attempt at local colour. The first act may be thought to suffer from this, but in the supernatural part the composer is completely successful. His Wilis have a character of their own, entirely distinct from that of any other operatic spectres. There is a fiendish rapture in their gambols, which Puccini has been very happy in conveying. The subject of "Le Villi" is perhaps scarcely suited for operatic purposes, and therefore the success which it has always met hitherto may be put down entirely to the merits of the music.

The favourable reception of " Le Villi " established Puccini's reputation in his own country. He became a marked man, and Italy learned to look upon him as one of the most promising composers of the rising generation. His next work, unfortunately, did not do much to increase his popularity. "Edgar" was produced at La Scala on the 21st of April 1889. It was not successful, although much of the music was scarcely

inferior to that of "Le Villi." The *libretto* was
a very tedious and undramatic affair, although
written by so experienced an author as Signor
Fontana. The heroine is a gipsy, a feebler
edition of Carmen, who beguiles the hero
from his village home to her mountain retreat.
He soon tires of this, and, like Tannhäuser,
breaks away from his siren and hurries to the
battle-field. He returns in the disguise of a
friar, and after abjuring the gipsy and her fatal
charms hopes to find repose in the arms of a
village maiden, the Micaela of the story, who
has loved him from the first. The gipsy,
however, contrives to stab her rival, who dies
in the hero's embrace, while the infuriated
crowd drag off her murderess to the scaffold.
The music of " Edgar " was probably affected by
the weakness of the *libretto*. Much of it was
melodious, but the portions intended to be
most impressive often ended in being merely
noisy, and the orchestration, though occasionally
brilliant and felicitous, was more often laboured
and affected. It would have been unfair to

expect much subtlety of characterisation from a composer called upon to deal with personages of so spectral an unreality as the *dramatis personæ* of " Edgar," and it must be owned that Puccini's music reflects only too faithfully the conventional types of the *libretto*. Altogether, there is little doubt that "Edgar," though a work of promise and talent, richly deserved to fail. So far as I know, it was never revived, and certainly has not been performed out of Italy.

After the failure of "Edgar" Puccini kept silence for some years, and when he did once more challenge the verdict of Milanese connoisseurs, he made it plain that his time had not been wasted. The eccentricities and exaggerations of " Edgar " had given place in " Manon Lescaut " to a style of singular strength and maturity.

" Manon Lescaut " is founded upon the Abbé Prévost's famous romance, but, as has often been already observed, it is really only a string of detached scenes, and would be absolutely un-

FACSIMILE OF AUTOGRAPH SCORE BY PUCCINI
"*Manon Lescaut*," *Act III., Canzone del Lampionaio*

intelligible to any one who was not previously familiar with the story. This defect is easily explained by the history of the *libretto* itself, which was the united work of the composer himself and several friends. The general impression which it conveys is that of having been written round the one really fine situation of the opera, namely the close of the third act. It was probably this scene, the departure of the *filles de ioie* for America, which originally fired the composer to attack the story, especially since it is not treated in Massenet's " Manon."

The first act deals with the meeting between the lovers at Amiens, and their flight to Paris. In the second act we find Manon installed as the mistress of Geronte di Lavoir, surrounded by crowds of admirers. Des Grieux penetrates to her apartment, and after a scene of passionate upbraiding persuades her to fly with him. But before they can depart they are interrupted by her irate protector, who in revenge summons the police and consigns Manon to St. Lazare.

The third act shows the Quay at Havre and the

embarkation of the *filles de joie* for New Orleans ; and the last act, which takes place in America, is one long duet between Manon and Des Grieux, ending with Manon's death.

Puccini's score is so full of beauties and is so exceedingly promising that it seems ungracious to point out its defects. But it has one inherent weakness, which is not to be lightly passed over. It is almost entirely deficient in characterisation. Manon and her lover are simply the ordinary hero and heroine of Italian opera. Call them what you will, the music would suit them equally well. So far as Des Grieux is concerned this is pardonable, for even the Abbé Prévost has not contrived to make him a very interesting creature. But with Manon the case is different. She lives and breathes in the Abbé's pages, and any treatment of her character which does not coincide with his is not merely wrong, it is impossible. Friendly critics tell us that we ought to put ourselves in Puccini's place, and look at Manon through Italian spectacles. It appears to me that this is precisely what we must not do. We must not

use spectacles at all, whether Italian, French, or
English. Verdi did not use spectacles in the
case of "Otello" or "Falstaff." He gave
us Shakespeare's characters pure and simple,
and for that reason his music is true and will
live ; while Puccini's, beautiful and passionate
as much of it is, will soon be forgotten.
Ambroise Thomas's "Hamlet" is another case
in point. French critics still insist that this
is a masterpiece. But we know our Shakespeare
too well to admit their claims. We know that
Shakespeare's Hamlet is the only possible one,
and it is because the French composer could
not work without his French spectacles, that his
work has never been accepted in countries
where "the divine Williams" is anything more
than a name.

Puccini was not the first to realise the operatic
possibilities of Manon. In 1856 Auber wrote
a "Manon Lescaut" to a *libretto* by Scribe,
which is now completely forgotten. Only one
morceau, a pretty "Chanson Bourbonnaise,"
survives and is still occasionally heard at

concerts. In 1884 was produced Massenet's " Manon," one of the most successful of modern French operas, and perhaps the most characteristic work of the brilliant composer.

I do not intend to institute an elaborate comparison between Massenet and Puccini, because in music comparisons of all sorts are elusive and unsatisfactory ; but the fact of both composers having treated the same subject makes it almost impossible to avoid mentioning their works side by side. The two operas, besides, illustrate rather curiously the strength and weakness of their respective schools. I do not think that Massenet could ever have written Puccini's third act, or anything like it, clever as he is, but in the lighter parts of the story he is far ahead.

Of course, the fact of his being a Frenchman gives him an immense advantage, but by the side of his dainty music Puccini sounds very ponderous. The truth is, that " Young Italy " is rather heavy-handed. It is so terribly in earnest that it has had no time to acquire the lighter graces of style. So I look upon Puccini's

first act and a good deal of the second—all
Manon's scene with the dancing master, for
instance, in which the composer's dogged determination to be light and sparkling is really
pathetic—as, comparatively speaking, a failure.
But when he comes to the more serious part of the
story he improves vastly. There is real passion
in the great duet, and the close of the scene, with
its vigorous *fugato*, is full of life. The third act is
masterly in conception. The scene is the quay at
Havre. Des Grieux and Lescaut are watching
under the windows of the prison in which Manon
and her wretched companions are immured, trying
in vain to devise some means of escape for the
poor prisoner. Through the bars of her window
Manon and her lover exchange passionate vows
of constancy. Morning dawns, and one by one
the unfortunate women are led out and conducted on board the ship which is to take them
to New Orleans. A crowd has collected, which
greets the poor wretches with mockery or sympathy, according to its changing temperament.
Des Grieux has been allowed to bid adieu to

Manon. Above the murmurs of the people the
voices of the lovers rise in a passionate farewell,
while the dull monotonous voice of the sergeant,
calling the names of the wretched women one
by one, sounds through the music like the knell
of a funeral bell. The scene is worked up to a
climax of great power. The women are all on
board, and the signal for weighing anchor is
about to be given, when Des Grieux breaks in
with one last appeal for mercy. The kindly
sergeant half relents, and as a compromise
allows him to accompany Manon to the shores
of the new world. This is the great scene of
the opera, and Puccini has treated it with
consummate pathos and with a complete know-
ledge of dramatic effect. He has shown that
he can treat the concerted *Finale*, which as a
rule we look upon as something altogether conventional and old-fashioned, with absolute truth
and dramatic realism. Intrinsically the scene is
superb, but after the curtain has fallen there
comes the question whether the dignity and
passion of this act are in keeping with the

character of Manon. Can a nature which is
au fond merely frivolous and pleasure-seeking
rise in adversity to nobility? In the pages of
the Abbé Prévost we find a different story.

"Hélas," répondit Manon, "une vie si mal-
heureuse mérite-t-elle le soin que nous en
prenons? Mourons au Havre, mon cher
chevalier. Que la mort finisse tout d'un coup
nos misères! Irons-nous les traîner dans un
pays inconnu, où nous devons nous attendre
sans doute à d'horribles extrémites, puisqu'on
a voulu m'en faire un supplice? Mourons, ou
du moins donne-moi la mort, et va chercher un
autre sort dans les bras d'une amante plus
heureuse."

This is the true Manon, the proper dramatic
contrast to the devoted and self-sacrificing Des
Grieux. Nevertheless, I confess that, when I
heard "Manon Lescaut" for the first time,
these considerations did not prevent me from
appreciating the beauty of Puccini's music.
It was not, in fact, until a distinguished
musician who happened to be present observed

that the third act reminded him of "Tristan und Isolde" that my slumbering conscience awoke.

What criticism in reality could be more damning than this? What possible connection is there between "Tristan" and "Manon Lescaut"? What quality have Manon and Isolde in common? If Puccini has really caught an echo of the splendid passion of Wagner, he stands self-convicted of a total misapprehension of the Abbé Prévost's luckless lovers.

In the last act of "Manon Lescaut" it appears to me that Puccini's inspiration breaks down. The scene is laid in a desert plain in America, where the lovers are wandering alone. Their duet, which ends with Manon's death, is very long, and after the exciting close of the third act seems rather an anti-climax. Melodically, too, it appears to me to be commonplace, and though the orchestra is cleverly treated, there is not enough dramatic material to enlist the attention.

Although the production of "Manon Lescaut"

in England was not a popular success, the remarkable promise of the score was amply recognised by all competent critics. Puccini is undoubtedly the most fully equipped of the younger generation of Italian composers. He has an undeniable gift of melody, strong dramatic power, a cultivated sense of orchestral colour, and little inclination for those sensational and meretricious tricks which are so often apparent in the work of his contemporaries. His power of characterisation is weak at present, but he is still a young man, and every one is not born a Mozart. It is said that Verdi has spoken of him as the most promising of his successors. However that may be, it is certain that the composer of " Le Villi " and " Manon Lescaut " possesses qualities which under the proper conditions ought to develop into something near akin to genius.

R. LEONCAVALLO

RUGGIERO LEONCAVALLO

MATTHEW ARNOLD tells a story in one of his essays of a friend of his, a Member of Parliament, who once shocked him very grievously by saying that he thought the fact of a thing being an anomaly was no objection to it whatever. I have always had a sneaking affection for the peccant M.P. and his paradox, and now I feel as though I had finally accepted his point of view by including Ruggiero Leoncavallo among the Masters of Italian Music. I certainly do not think him as yet entitled to the position of a Master, but in summing up the history of modern Italian music, his is a name which cannot well be left out; firstly, because his " Pagliacci " is one of the most successful operas

of the last few years; and secondly, because
Leoncavallo, like Boito, is not only a musician
but a man of letters as well, and, besides writing
his own *libretti*, has promulgated a profession of
artistic faith, which to the future historian of
" Young Italy " may prove to be a document of
some importance.

As regards his music (and indeed the remark
applies equally well to all the music of the
youthful Italians, who at the present moment
have got the ear of Europe) it is early as yet
to speak with any degree of decision. Whether
we are face to face with a new development of
opera, a combination of German polyphony and
Italian melody, which will revolutionise the
history of the art, or whether " Young Italy,"
with all its claims and pretensions is a mere
bubble destined to break in an hour, the wisest
of us can hardly pretend to decide offhand.
The three musicians upon whom the hopes of
Italy are chiefly centred are still young, and
what they may in time become, a generation
which has seen the development of Wagner and

Verdi can scarcely pretend to predict. So far, we can only judge by what they have given us.

Ruggiero Leoncavallo was born in Naples on the 8th of March 1858. His musical education began with the pianoforte. His first master was named Siri. Afterwards he learnt from Simonetti, a musician who may be known to a few English students as the compiler of an " Enciclopedia del Pianista." Leoncavallo learnt harmony as well as the piano from Simonetti, and afterwards completed his studies in the former with Professor Ruta.

In the fulness of time Leoncavallo entered the Naples Conservatoire, where his studies progressed favourably under various masters, whose names would certainly not interest English readers. One of them, however, Lauro Rossi, a composer who had occasional successes at the theatre, may be mentioned as the first to direct his pupil's thoughts to the field of opera, in which he was afterwards to win his most important triumphs. When his studies at Naples were finished, Leoncavallo—in whom the man of etters was always as much to the fore as the musician—went to Bologna, attracted by the lectures of the famous poet Carducci. There he wrote his first opera, " Tommaso Chatterton," a work which has not as yet seen the light. In Bologna, Leoncavallo experienced the first of a series of disappointments which would have crushed a man of less perseverance and determination. He arranged with an *impresario* for the production of his opera, and with the guilelessness of youth paid him a large sum for the necessary expenses. The manager promptly decamped, leaving the unlucky "Tommaso Chatterton" in the hands of the composer, where it has remained ever since. Leoncavallo was thus thrown on his own resources, but he was not the man to sit down under his disappointment. For many years he had to work, and to work hard. He travelled all over Europe, giving piano and singing lessons where he could. He visited England, France, Germany, Holland, and even Egypt. Everywhere he met with disappointment and hardship, but he was animated by one great idea, which sustained him in all his reverses. He had made up his mind to set the Renaissance to music— to construct a gigantic Trilogy which should rival Wagner's "Nibelungen." Instead of mythology it should deal with history; it should be Italian instead of German. The idea was a noble one, but the task would have been crushing to any but a musical genius of the first water, a man of wide theatrical experience, and a poet, all rolled into one.

After many years' wandering, Leoncavallo presented himself at Milan with the plan of his Trilogy complete, and the *libretto* of the first part, "I Medici," already written. The publishing house of Ricordi saw his MS., and agreed to produce the work. The music was written in a year, and the opera, except for the orchestration, was ready for production. Then came the delays and postponements which seem inseparable from the *coulisses* of an opera-house. Three years passed, and still "I Medici" had not been performed. Then in despair Leoncavallo betook himself to the rival publisher, Sonzogno. Here he met with a far more cordial reception. One interview gave birth to the idea of "Pagliacci," a two-act opera for which Leoncavallo wrote both words and music. This was produced on the 21st of May 1892, with complete and instantaneous success. Sonzogno lost no time in acquiring "I Medici" from Ricordi, and this was produced at the Dal Verme Theatre in November 1893.

"Pagliacci" is the most successful of the operas which may be ascribed to the success of "Cavalleria Rusticana." To a certain extent it reproduces the features which contributed to the success of its predecessor. The scene is laid in humble life, the main hinges of the story are love, adultery, and murder; the action is concise and the conclusion tragic. The personages of the story are a troupe of travelling comedians called *Pagliacci*, such as may often be seen in Italian villages. They perambulate the country, going from fair to fair, playing the old story of Colombine, Harlequin and Punchinello, in any

rustic theatres that may be available, before open-
mouthed audiences of *contadini*. The story of
" Pagliacci " begins with the arrival of one of
these troupes in a country village. We soon
find out that all is not in harmony in the little
company. Tonio (the Taddeo, or Clown)
loves Nedda (Colombine), the wife of Canio
(Pagliaccio), but she already has a lover in the
shape of a young peasant named Silvio, and
rejects the clumsy advances of the other with
scorn. Tonio overhears the mutual vows of
Nedda and her lover, and, bent on vengeance,
hastens off to bring the unsuspecting Canio
upon the scene. He only arrives in time to see
the disappearance of Silvio, and cannot terrify
his wife into disclosing the name of her lover,
though he is only just stopped by Beppe, the
Harlequin of the troupe, from stabbing her on
the spot. The second act is on the evening of
the same day, a few hours later. The curtain of
the rustic theatre goes up and the little play
begins. By a curious coincidence the mimic
tragedy represents exactly the real situation of

the action. Colombine is entertaining her lover
Harlequin in the absence of her husband
Pagliaccio, while Taddeo keeps a look-out for his
return. When he appears we soon see that what
was begun in jest is to finish in earnest. Canio
scarcely makes a pretence of keeping to the *rôle*
of Pagliaccio. Mad with jealousy, he rushes on
his wife and tries to make her confess the name
of her lover. She refuses, and in the end he
stabs her, while Silvio, who has made one of the
rustic audience, rushes on to the stage only to
receive his death-blow as well. As the curtain
falls Canio cries, though sometimes the tag is
given to Tonio, "La commedia è finita." The
plot of "Pagliacci" bears a striking resemblance
to a tale by Catulle Mendès, "La Femme de
Tabarin." This similarity has given rise to a
rather acrimonious discussion between the
respective authors, *et adhuc sub judice lis est*.
However, though the idea is a good one, it is by
no means impossible that it may have occurred
independently both to the French and Italian
littérateurs, and this is certainly the simplest

solution of the difficulty. What I have said about "Cavalleria Rusticana" applies equally well to "Pagliacci." The theme is squalid and unpleasant, it is true, but it is so simple and straightforward that it makes an excellent subject for an opera. Italian critics have made sundry objections to the diction of the poem. The language, they say, is far too refined for strolling players, but this is not likely to trouble an English audience very seriously. As regards the score it is impossible to speak so favourably. At its best the music is merely an inoffensive though superfluous accompaniment to the action of the plot; at its worst it is unoriginal, vulgar, and pretentious. Leoncavallo is at a great disadvantage as compared with Mascagni. He is nothing of a melodist, and to make up for his lack of invention he is forced to fall back upon his memory. " Pagliacci " is full of reminiscences. Not only is the influence of other composers very marked throughout the score, but many of the tunes are palpably secondhand articles. *C'est imiter quelqu'un que de planter des choux,* of course, and I have not the shadow of a doubt that Leoncavallo appropriates quite unconsciously—otherwise how could he have fixed on "When other lips" as his love-motive? But at the same time, his lack of originality detracts sorely from the value of his work. But even when his tunes are his own, they are generally the most commonplace affair imaginable, though he has a clever trick of dressing them out with piquant effects of orchestration; witness Nedda's *Ballatella*, in which the fanciful accompaniment goes far to cover the poverty of the melody.

There is in fact a good deal of cleverness in "Pagliacci," which may for a time deceive even the very elect as to the true value of the score. The last scene is particularly ingenious. Canio's passionate denunciations stand out so forcibly from the background formed by the Minuet and Gavotte which have been associated with the little play, and the whole situation is so effective, that one almost forgets to wonder what possible connection there can be between a sordid little troupe of Italian mountebanks and the delicate

grace of a Gavotte or Minuet. " Pagliacci " is
undoubtedly effective, and even clever, up to
a certain point, and so long as the modern
passion for one-act melodramas continues it will
probably have its little day of success; but
Leoncavallo himself would probably deprecate
any serious criticism of his talents founded
upon it, and would prefer to be judged by " I
Medici," a work in which he has put forth his
full powers.

The idea of a Trilogy dealing with the Italian
Renaissance had long been Leoncavallo's darling
project. The score of " I Medici " had lain for
many years in his portfolio. At last the success
of " Pagliacci " smoothed away all the difficulties
which had previously hindered its presentment.
The ambitious composer was at length to appear
in his true colours, not as one of the petty
tribe fostered by an ephemeral taste for squalid
sensationalism, but as a magician who could
conjure to life the dead heroes of the glowing
past. Lest there should be any doubt as to the
extreme importance of the position which " I

Medici " was to occupy in the history of Italian music, the author wrote a letter to Dr. Tonolla, the musical critic of *La Sera*, in which he detailed the theory upon which he had worked and the aims which he had in view. This letter I reproduce :

MY DEAR TONOLLA,

You can understand the emotion I feel in sending you my poem. It is seventeen years since I first confided my great project to your sympathetic ears. I was then a boy, and had my full share of the enthusiasm and ignorance of youth. I had, however, even then enough common sense to see that I needed much study before I undertook such work, and I did study *con amore*, notwithstanding my sufferings and privations. I passed nights without sleep and days without food, but I always kept my ideal before me.

And now the goal is reached, the work is done, and you have come to Milan to hear "I Medici." I ask the hospitality of your paper for this letter so that there may be no doubt as to the purpose of my work.

> " On va s'imaginer que c'est une préface
> Moi qui n'en lis jamais. . . . ."

So wrote Musset, and I think it better to follow his example and tell you in a few words what my idea was in writing "I Medici," than to burden the *libretto* with a preface which nobody would read.

I wished, then, to try a new kind of poem, new at any rate to the lyric stage—the Epic.

Why should not music have its epic, possessing as it does the language most fitted to it, and more poetical than poetry itself?

Having decided to write epic music, I began to think about my subject.

I had also to reconcile this idea with my love for realism in literature and in art, because for me music is the most poetical and perfect expression of the mind.

To get the necessary inspiration I wanted living subjects, with flesh and bones, like myself, who should feel and think like men and women.

who should suffer from the same passions that sway our own hearts and senses. I decided, therefore, to take my epic from history. I sought in the contemporary chronicles for the characters, the passions, the weaknesses and the crimes of heroes as they really existed. To bring to life a whole epoch! To multiply the miracle of Lazarus, and command the tombs to give up their dead! To seek for the philosophical link subsisting between events which seem unconnected, but are in reality the logical productions of one scheme of life and politics. All this tempted me, and I said to myself: "So much the worse for you if the burden is too heavy for your back, and if the ruins of the vast buildings crush you. But at least you will die honourably."

Machiavelli's "Florentine History" inspired me with the first idea of this work. Then I began to study in earnest, and I read as much as possible of what has been written about this period. Besides the immense mass of material which I found in the libraries of Florence,

Rome, and Bologna, I studied standard modern
works most religiously, such as Villari's "Machiavelli" and "Savonarola," and Carducci's splendid
prefaces to the poems of Politian and Lorenzo
de' Medici. Yes, Boileau is right : "Rien n'est
beau que le vrai !" What a wide field for the
artist, for the philosopher, and for the historian
is this glorious period of Italian history—the
Renaissance ! "Quanto sangue e quanto fango
a rimescolare," as Carducci says. After carefully studying this period of history, I decided
in favour of a Trilogy, because I thought it the
only form in which I could reproduce my idea
on the stage. I subdivided the historical periods
in the following way : First part, "I Medici,"
from the accession of Sixtus IV. to the Pazzi
Conspiracy; second part, "Savonarola," from
the investiture of Fra Benedetto to the death of
Savonarola ; third part, "Cesare Borgia," from
the death of the Duke of Candia to that of
Alexander VI. I have scrupulously respected
the historical characters, keeping faithful to the
customs, manners, and even to the language of

the times. With the exception of some slight anachronisms required by a theatrical performance, I shall present men and their actions as they are described by contemporary historians. Running parallel to these historical portraits is this philosophic idea : the statesman of the Renaissance, recognising the instability of government based on popular favour, seeks an ally in the Church, which betrays him, and he, fired with overweening ambition and mistrustful of everybody and everything, becomes at last Cesare Borgia. The title of the Trilogy was suggested by that of Wagner's " Götterdämmerung." For a moment I thought of borrowing from my master his whole title, for his little gods— Wotan, Donner, and the rest—are pigmies beside Lorenzo de' Medici, Savonarola, Cesare Borgia, Alexander VI., and Machiavelli. I have, however, selected the title " Crepusculum " because it is more poetical and more practical. What I have made of it my music will show in a few days. I will only add that, faithful to the maxims of the great Bayreuth master, I have

sought to make my poem a national one, and
I have surrounded it with an atmosphere of
Italianism. And, now, *alea jacta est.* This
work which, like a favourite child, I have nursed
and fondled for many years, I now leave alone
upon the highway, exposed to the attacks of
the critics. I dare to hope that it will be strong
enough to defend itself. As for me, my task is
finished—in this First Part—my only comfort
in these terribly anxious days being that I have
done all I was able to do. If, notwithstanding
all my care, I have not succeeded, it will not
be for want of trying, and I shall repeat with
the poet Musset:

" Mon verre n'est pas grand, mais je bois dans
mon verre."

Tibi,

R. LEONCAVALLO.

The wisdom of publishing this manifesto was
doubtful. It was mercilessly satirised in Milan.
and even an indulgent critic might have been
pardoned for murmuring :

" Quid dignum tanto feret hic promissor hiatu ? "

But it established one point effectually. Leoncavallo did not wish his opera to be criticised from any but the most lofty standpoint. He intended to write an Italian " Ring der Nibelungen," and begged every one to bear that fact in mind. Under these circumstances there is only one possible verdict. "I Medici" is a complete failure. Judged as an ordinary melodrama there is much to be said for it. It contains some effective scenes, and one genuinely dramatic moment. The music is the work of an extremely clever man. It is seldom original, it is true, indeed it teems with the most audacious plagiarisms; but it is cleverly strung together, and the orchestration is full of fancy and even imagination. Nevertheless, as a serious work of art its value is absolutely *nil*. It is the work of a cultivated student of contemporary music, a man who has read and digested the best scores of the best musicians of Europe during the last fifty years. It is a brilliant exercise, a triumph of musical eclecticism; but as empty of all real inspiration as one of Caracci's Holy Families.

The subject of " I Medici " is the Pazzi conspiracy, which was directed against the persons
of Lorenzo and Giuliano de' Medici. Designed
to overthrow the Medici power in Florence, it
succeeded only in establishing it more firmly
than ever. Giuliano was assassinated in the
church of Santa Reparata, but Lorenzo almost
miraculously escaped the daggers of the conspirators, and executed a bloody though well-
deserved vengeance upon one and all of them.

So far as the actual conspiracy is concerned,
Leoncavallo adheres closely to history. In the
treatment of his characters he allows himself
more latitude, but no one will quarrel with him
upon that account. He certainly could not
have chosen an epoch for his opera more rich
in colour and life than fifteenth-century Florence,
or a hero and heroine more picturesque than
Giuliano de' Medici and Simonetta Cattánei.
Giuliano is the ideal knight of the Italian
chroniclers. In the pages of Politian he lives
as a mediæval Hippolytus, a stainless youth
who shuns the charms of woman and delights

only in wars and the chase. Simonetta is one of the most fascinating figures of the Renaissance. Sung by Bernardo Pulci and painted by Botticelli, she moves through that wonderful world like a queen of romance. Her beauty was the boast of Italy, and her early death drew an elegy from every poet in Florence.

The first act of "I Medici" shows her meeting with Giuliano in the woods. The scene is founded upon a famous passage in the *Giostra* of Politian. Throughout the opera Leoncavallo has taken extraordinary pains to model his diction upon the language of the fifteenth century. Italian critics are not slow to point out instances of intrusive modernism and even locutions borrowed from nineteenth-century France, but it hardly becomes an Englishman to attempt to penetrate these mysteries. Much of the *libretto* is written in polished and flowing verse and, under the circumstances, Leoncavallo's archaic spelling, and even the erudite footnotes with which his pages bristle, may be easily condoned. The second act introduces the conspirators, who assemble in the Piazza di Santa Trinità in Florence to concert their plans. There is a good deal of rather purposeless serenading and merry-making later in the act, and the curtain falls upon a declaration of love by Fioretta, Simonetta's friend and *confidante*, to the astonished Giuliano.

In the third act we might almost fancy ourselves back in " Rigoletto." On the left of the stage is Simonetta's house, and on the right, across the street, we see a section of Fioretta's dwelling. Fioretta has become Giuliano's mistress, but the latter still retains a more than friendly interest in the unfortunate Simonetta, who is dying of consumption. This is a violation of historic truth which is hardly just to Giuliano's character. Simonetta in reality died some years before her lover's assassination. He did, it is true, subsequently console himself with the affections of another lady, who bore him the child which afterwards became Pope Clement VII., but there is no reason to suppose that he was untrue to Simonetta during her lifetime.

Nevertheless, dramatic exigencies are inexorable, and in the pages of " I Medici " he emulates the hero of Peacock's " Nightmare Abbey " in his capacity for being in love with two women at the same time.

After a monologue from Fioretta in which we are put *au fait* with the situation, Giuliano appears, dogged by the conspirators. He enters Fioretta's house, while Simonetta appears at her own doorway, which is conveniently placed for overhearing the plotting in the street. There she is discovered by Montesecco, one of the conspirators, who shows her through a window her faithless lover in the arms of Fioretta. In spite of his perfidy, she resolves to warn him of the plot against his life, which she has overheard. Worn out, however, by disease and anguish, she drops dead at his feet without being able to articulate the precious tidings, and the curtain falls upon Montesecco's impressive words, " E dunque Iddio che i Medici a morte condannò."

The fourth act is another proof of the fact that if real events are put upon the stage exactly as

they occurred, they make no effect whatever.
Probably the last tableau of "I Medici" is a
very fair reproduction of the famous scene in
the church of Santa Reparata. The stage is
crowded with Florentines of every rank and
station. The conspirators mix with the people
and talk together in low voices while the choir
chants a "Credo." Suddenly Pazzi plunges a
dagger into Giuliano's heart, while two priests
endeavour unsuccessfully to assassinate Lorenzo. .
For a time all is confusion, but after a short
interval the latter comes forward—this, of course,
really took place outside the church—and
addresses the people. He tells them of the
deeds of his ancestors, and speedily wins their
allegiance. They rush out with shouts of
vengeance, and Lorenzo is left beside the dead
body of Giuliano crying, " Io regno alfin."

So much for the *libretto*. As regards the
music, there is no need for elaborate description.
The score of "I Medici" has been made the
subject of an exhaustive analysis in the pages of

the "Rivistà Musicale," in which the author, Signor Giani, has been at immense pains to trace the various sources from which Leoncavallo has drawn inspiration. Wagner, Verdi, Schumann, and Meyerbeer, all have been laid under contribution. Indeed, Signor Giani appears not to have left a stone unturned in his endeavours to prove his countryman a plagiarist. He does not, of course, accuse Leoncavallo of voluntarily appropriating other men's tunes. No one in his senses would consciously take a well-known motive from "Siegfried" as the principal theme of his love duet. However, there it stands naked and unashamed in the first act of "I Medici," and throughout the score there are many other instances of appropriation no less patent. But the important point is not that a melody here and there has been borrowed from some other composer, but that Leoncavallo appears as yet not to have developed any style peculiar to himself. Sometimes he is Wagnerian, sometimes Meyerbeerian, sometimes Verdian, according to the situation which he has to treat. In the idyllic passages of the first act, the influence of Wagner is strongest. The texture of the score, the contrast of sonorities, the harmonic progressions, all breathe the potent influence of the composer of the "Waldweben." The conspirators suggested Meyerbeer, and accordingly in the second act we find passages which might have been taken bodily from the pages of "Le Prophète" or "Les Huguenots." In the third act the influence of "Rigoletto" was not to be resisted. The associations suggested by the pair of lovers inside the house, with the cast-off mistress in the street outside, were too strong for Leoncavallo's individuality, and we have a concerted piece which might have been written by Verdi. This, be it noted, original or not, is far and away the most effective part of the opera, a fact which suggests that Leoncavallo is happiest, not as a revolutionist bent upon the complete reformation of Italian opera, but when working upon the established melodramatic lines so dear to his countrymen.

The one point in "I Medici" which may be

fully and unreservedly praised is the orchestration, which is not only intrinsically beautiful, but shows a strong feeling for characterisation. For the rest, it will be best to dismiss "I Medici" as the work of a composer who has not yet found his feet. The plagiarisms which disfigure it may only show that Leoncavallo has not yet emerged from that fluid condition of mind in which Wagner wrote "Die Feen" and "Das Liebes-verbot." The various elements which are so strangely at war with one another in "I Medici" may yet combine to form an artistic personality of which Italy will have reason to be proud.

Since the production of "I Medici," Leon-cavallo has only given the world an orchestral piece with chorus, founded upon Balzac's "Seraphita." This was produced at Milan last summer with success. It is understood that he has been requested by the Emperor of Germany to write an opera upon a Prussian subject, "Roland of Berlin," a mark of favour to a foreign composer which has naturally been re-ceived in Germany without much enthusiasm.

Leoncavallo's next opera will be looked for with much interest by those who, like myself, believe that when he has assimilated the various external influences which have hitherto only served to disturb his individuality, he will produce work of real and permanent value.

SOME OTHER ITALIAN COMPOSERS

THE difficulties in the way of writing a chapter upon the condition of instrumental music in modern Italy are almost as formidable as in the case of the celebrated treatise on snakes in Iceland. There was a time when Italy led the van in this department of art as in every other. Vivaldi, Corelli, and Scarlatti were giants in their day, but since their time abstract music has pined and faded in the land of song, until in the earlier years of this century it had practically ceased to exist. Cherubini, though exiled from his native country, revived the best traditions of Italian instrumental music. He deserved to be the founder of a new school, for his music (particularly his string quartets), though strictly classical in form, had a very marked individuality. But the good seed fell on barren soil, and he left no successor to carry on his work. It would not be difficult to trace the reasons for the scanty favour shown to instrumental music in Italy. There is something in the Italian nature—we may call it fervour or superficiality as we like—to which the form and science of instrumental music are repellent. From the very first, Italy decided that opera was the truest expression of her musical life, and as year by year opera absorbed more completely the attention and talents of her musicians, abstract music sank into the background. In Germany the reverse happened. There the seed sown by the Italian instrumental writers fell on good ground, and a body of musicians sprang up who soon distanced their venerable predecessors south of the Alps. Opera, however, remained more or less an exotic for many years; indeed it was not until the time of Weber that Germany could claim the possession of a distinctively national operatic type.

In our own time the state of affairs, at any
rate in Italy, is not much changed. Here and
there in the peninsula are composers who have
devoted their energies partially or entirely to
the composition of abstract music. But in no
sense is there an Italian school of instrumental
music. That is to say, the music produced by
these composers has no conclusively Italian
stamp: it is, as a rule, generated by careful
and intelligent study of the works of German
composers. As examples of Italian instrumental
composers I have chosen Giovanni Sgambati
and Antonio Bazzini. They are certainly the
most distinguished cultivators of this branch
of art, but it is only just to say that their reputation is at least as much due to the absence of
competition as to their own intrinsic merits.
This sounds rather unkind, but it is as well
to realise at the outset that neither of these
excellent men can pretend to rank with the
great composers even of our own day. Sgambati
and Bazzini both began as performers, the former upon the piano, the latter upon the violin.

Both won reputations, which may almost be called European, in their respective *métiers*. Both, too, began to compose at an early age. As was only natural, the style of their earlier works was strongly affected by the instruments which they cultivated, and consequently the musical value of these youthful effusions is not great. Later in life both composers to a great extent gave up concert work and devoted themselves almost wholly to teaching and composition. From this time forward, the merit of their works increased vastly. It is no exaggeration to say that the music which they have written since their retirement from the world of *virtuosi* is singularly free from that touch of insincerity and showiness which so often taints the best work of the *virtuoso*-composer to the end of his days.

Giovanni Sgambati is by no means an unfamiliar figure in London concert-rooms. He has several times paid visits to England, and has figured as pianist and conductor both at

St. James's Hall and at the Crystal Palace. Apart from his musical talents, Sgambati has a special claim upon our sympathies, for he is himself half an Englishman, his mother being the daughter of Joseph Gott, the sculptor. He was born at Rome on May 28th, 1843, and at a very early age evinced a strong taste for music. His precociousness must have been something quite out of the common, for his father, who died in 1849, was induced by these juvenile manifestations of musical genius to relinquish his scheme of training his son to his own profession of the Law.

After the death of Sgambati the elder, his widow moved to the little Umbrian town of Trevi, where she soon married again, and in that out-of-the-way corner of Italy the youthful Giovanni contrived, *tant bien que mal*, to pick up such scraps of musical instruction as the place afforded. He composed, of course, but his first efforts, oddly enough, had nothing to do with the piano, the instrument which was subsequently to make him famous. He devoted

himself at first to sacred music, but his youthful
productions have never been published. In
1860 he left Trevi, and established himself in
Rome, where he became known as a promising
pianist. Instrumental music was at that time
in so little favour in Italy, that to be a pianist
and nothing more was something quite unusual. But Sgambati's eccentricity carried him
to even greater lengths. He was a staunch
exponent of German music, and his playing
of Beethoven, Chopin, and Schumann soon
became famous. But though the elect gathered
round him, it is not to be supposed that the
conservative element in Roman music looked
upon the young revolutionist so favourably.
The musical atmosphere of Italy in the sixties
was eminently anti-Teutonic, and Sgambati
had to put up with many rebuffs and much
determined opposition in his passage towards
the light.

When even the weighty Fétis (or, to be ac-
curate, his successor and supplementer) sneers
at him as the grand apostle of the music of the

future and a man given over to exaggeration and
extravagance, it is not to be wondered at that the
journalists of Rome found expressions even less
complimentary with which to brand the audacious
innovator. Sgambati had determined to leave
so uncongenial an environment, and had even
made up his mind to start for Germany, when
the arrival of Liszt in Rome induced him to
change his mind. Liszt had made Weimar too
hot to hold him. The bad feeling stirred up by
his production of Cornelius's "Barber of Bagdad"
had compelled him finally to turn his back upon
the place. He found his way to Rome by the
end of the year 1861, and in the voluminous
correspondence which he kept up with German,
French, and English friends we soon begin to
meet with the name of Sgambati. At first Liszt
found Roman society "attractive if not exactly
musical," and spent most of his time working at
his oratorio, "St. Elisabeth." Soon, however, all
that was best in Roman musical life began to
collect around the person of the great musician.
In August 1862 he writes : "I have fished out here

a very talented young pianist, Sgambati by name, who makes a first-rate partner in duets, and who, for example, plays the Dante Symphony boldly and correctly. It would be a pleasure to me to be able to go through the whole cycle of the Symphonic Poems with him." A year later he writes to his publishers for copies of his own " Etudes d'exécution transcendante " for Sgambati's benefit, who was to introduce them to the Roman public, "and he is fully competent to do so." From the same letter I cull a sentence, which throws a strange light upon the practical side of music in Rome at this time. "As it has been impossible for me to hunt out here a copyist who will fulfil the conditions that may reasonably be exacted (the one whom I employed pretty much last year divides his time between the prison and the public-house !), I am compelled to send you the manuscript, such as it is, with many apologies for its badly written appearance."

Liszt's friendship was invaluable to Sgambati. They worked together almost daily, and the

young man inbibed to the full his teacher's
enthusiasm for the noblest forms of art. In the
winter of 1864–65 Sgambati gave four orchestral
concerts, which, as Liszt bears witness, "had a
success both of fashion and good taste." At
this time, spurred on by Liszt's generous encouragement, Sgambati began to compose in
earnest. In 1864 he wrote a String Quartet;
in 1866 a Pianoforte Quintet; in 1867 an Octet,
a second Pianoforte Quintet, an Overture, and
other works. Meanwhile the work of evangel-
ising the Eternal City, musically speaking, proceeded apace. Sgambati was the leading spirit,
and under his direction concerts of orchestral
and chamber music became matters of common occurrence in Rome. In January 1868
Liszt writes : "Sgambati and Pinelli announce
six *matinées* of chamber music every Wednes-
day. The audience will be more numerous
this year than formerly. People are beginning
to talk about these *matinées* in the aristocratic
salons in which it is often *de bon ton* not to
listen to good music." A few days later he

adds : "Sgambati's *matinées* for chamber music
are better attended than ever this winter. They
include all that is musically interesting as regards
Rome." "Sgambati is very much in fashion
this winter, and the fashion is perfectly right in
this." Here is Liszt's private opinion of his protégé confided to Herr Brendel, the editor of
the *Allgemeine Musikalische Zeitung:* "Sgambati
is decidedly not an artist for a *watering-place*,
although as a *virtuoso* his talent is extraordinary
and undoubtedly effective. He plays Bach,
Beethoven, Chopin, Schumann, and my most
troublesome things, with perfect independence
and in a masterly style. His artistic tendencies
and sympathies are altogether ' new German.' "

In the spring of 1868 Sgambati gave some
concerts in Florence with Wilhelmj, the violinist ;
and in the following year he went with Liszt to
Germany, and was present at the production of
Wagner's " Das Rheingold " at Munich in July.
On his return to Rome, though Liszt was no
longer present to inspire him, he continued his
concerts in the same indefatigable way. There

is little to say regarding Sgambati's subsequent career. It consists chiefly of years of quiet work in Rome, varied by the production of compositions which, if unequal in merit, have at any rate sustained his reputation for a loftiness of aim and a mastery of musical science now as rare as they once were common in his country. In 1878 he was chosen Professor of the Piano at the Academy of Saint Cecilia at Rome, a position he has held ever since. His first Symphony (in D) was performed for the first time in 1881 at a concert in the Quirinal, in the presence of the King and Queen of Italy. It has been sometimes spoken of as the first Symphony, in the modern sense of the term, written by an Italian. Cherubini, as is well known, wrote one Symphony at the request of our own Philharmonic Society, but there is a possibility that this was only an expansion of a previously-written Quartet. However that may be, Sgambati's work was a great success. It was performed at the Crystal Palace the following year under the composer's own direction, and was very well received. It is thoroughly melodious, and written with complete command of all modern orchestral resources, but is not in any sense great. Indeed, its tunefulness occasionally degenerates into triviality, as in the case of a rather feeble little Serenade which ushers in the *Finale*. During this visit to England, Sgambati played his Pianoforte Concerto in G minor at a Philharmonic Concert. This performance was more of a success for the executant than the composer. The Concerto is a showy affair, strongly impregnated with the influence of Liszt, as indeed is only natural, but with little else to recommend it except a delightfully simple Romance which does duty for a slow movement. It cannot be said that Sgambati's visit to England resulted in instantaneous popularity for his music. It was not until 1890 that the Popular Concerts opened their doors to his Chamber Music. His Pianoforte Quintet in B flat (Op. 5) was then performed. It is an eminently attractive and well-written work, with a delightfully breezy

Barcarole as its second movement, which gives it a kind of national stamp. For the rest, the first and last movements are straightforward pieces of writing ; while the Andante, which is on a more elaborate scale, often rises to real passion. Strangely enough, it has never been performed again at the Popular Concerts, although its reception was exceedingly cordial. In 1891, Sgambati visited England once more, and gave a concert entirely of his own works, a most impolitic proceeding, which put the affection of even his warmest admirers to an uncommonly severe test. During this visit, too, he conducted his third Symphony at one of the Philharmonic Society's Concerts. This work was written in honour of the wedding of the Duke of Aosta in 1888, and is, therefore, known as the " Sinfonia Epitalamio." It is little more than a " pièce d'occasion," and is certainly far inferior both in scope and execution to the first Symphony. It is in three sections, entitled respectively, " In Church," " In the Garden," and " At Court." The scoring is clever and sonorous, but the work is scarcely of symphonic rank, and the sooner it is forgotten the better it will be for Sgambati's reputation. The second Symphony has never been performed in England, though it was selected by the Tonkünstler-Versammlung for performance, under the composer's direction, at Cologne in 1887. A so-called Te Deum for orchestra from his pen was performed at the Crystal Palace last year without much success.

Sgambati, in fine, is an admirable composer of the second rank. His mixed nationality and Italo-German training have given him wide and cosmopolitan sympathies, but he has no distinctive style, and his work is often marred by an obvious straining after effect. He is, perhaps, at his best in his compositions for the pianoforte, the instrument to which he owed his first successes in the world of music. These are often heard in our concert-rooms, and there is every likelihood of their being remembered when his symphonies and quintets have, as Mr. Swinburne puts it, "gone the way of all waxwork."

Antonio Bazzini was born at Brescia in 1818.
His family was an old one, and had numbered
among its members many musicians of distinction. One of his ancestors, Francesco Bazzini
(1600-1660), was a famous theorist and composer. He lived at the Court of the Duke of
Mantua, and was also heard at Vienna. He
wrote Sonatas for the theorbo and Canzonets for
a solo voice. It is said that he was also the
composer of an Oratorio, "La Rappresentaz-
ione di S. Orsola." Scarcely less famous was
another of the same family, probably a brother,
who died in 1639. He published, principally at
Venice, many volumes of masses and motets.
In spite of these distinguished ancestors, Antonio
Bazzini's own parents do not seem to have been
gifted with much musical taste. Fortunately for
his future, however, he had a godfather, a lawyer
named Buccelleni, who was clever enough to
detect the germs of talent in the little boy.
Buccelleni was himself a poet and an amateur of
the fine arts generally, and he did the wisest
thing possible under the circumstances. He

introduced the boy to a client of his own, Faustino Camisani, a violinist of some reputation, who we may presume undertook his musical education. At any rate, at the age of eighteen we find him installed as organist in the church of San Filippo at Brescia, giving performances of orchestral works of his own composition. In 1836 he played before Paganini, who was enraptured with his performance, and four years later, already famous as a *virtuoso* in Milan and the cities of Northern Italy, he undertook a tour which embraced most of the principal towns of Germany and Austria, the sinews of war being supplied by his godfather. He was absent from Italy six years, and it is to this period and to the classic influence of the German capitals in which he sojourned that his countrymen attribute the formation of his style, a happy combination of Italian melody and Teutonic science. His success was everywhere very great, and on his return to Italy he lost no time in setting forth upon another tour. This time his own country was the scene of his labours. He visited in turn Turin, Genoa, Florence, Rome, and Naples, and everywhere his playing excited the same enthusiasm. Then followed another tour in Spain and France. He played in Paris in 1852, and subdued even that critical audience by the dash and brilliancy of his method. After this final triumph, Bazzini devoted himself less to his violin and more and more to composition. In January 1867 an opera from his pen, "Turanda," was given at La Scala, but without success. Friendly critics attributed its failure to the weakness of the *libretto*, but there is nothing in Bazzini's music which gives the least indication of a talent for the stage. Bazzini was now established in Milan. After the failure of "Turanda," he wisely forswore the theatre and devoted himself almost entirely to chamber and symphonic music. He was looked upon as the leading representative of classicism in Italian music, and as such he was nominated in 1873 to the Professorship of Composition in the Conservatoire of Milan, as successor to Alberte Mazzucato, the master of

Boito. His success in this position was so very marked that in 1882 he was chosen to fill the vacant post of Director. Under his sway the Conservatoire has enjoyed golden days. Bazzini's wide sympathies and great erudition would in any country have marked him out as a man specially fitted for an important post of this kind; but in Italy, where musical taste is so often narrowed to a tiny groove, he was above all others the right man in the right place. Bazzini clings to the traditions of the ancients, and Bach and Beethoven are the gods of his special idolatry; but he is no mere pedant, and so far from ignoring the claims of more modern composers, he prides himself on being familiar with the works of Schumann and Brahms, Liszt and Wagner.

The list of Bazzini's own works is the best proof of the eclectic nature of his talent. He has touched almost every province of his art, and seldom without some success. His larger works, such as oratorios and symphonies, have not, so far as I know, reached our shores, but such opportunities as have occurred of hearing his music have generally resulted in giving a favourable impression of Bazzini's powers. In 1893 one of his String Quartets was performed at the Popular Concerts, which may be taken as a fair specimen of his style. It is transparently simple in construction, but is written with complete knowledge of the quartet form, and is throughout informed with a thoroughly Haydnesque geniality. It is unfortunate that except for this work we Londoners know Bazzini best by the show violin pieces of his younger days. These are still favoured by violinists; Señor Sarasate, in particular, often plays some of them. They are clever and effective, but have very little musical value. But if Bazzini's name is to live at all, it will be less as a composer than as a teacher. The influence of his ripe scholarship and wide musical sympathies upon the rising generation of Italian musicians can hardly be over-estimated. It has indeed borne fruit already in the works of many who have sat at his feet in the Conservatoire, and it is perhaps not too much to say that his influence has materially helped to model the future of Italian music.

But for his early and lamented death in 1891, Franco Faccio might have been bracketed with his friend Luigi Mancinelli as a representative pair of composer-conductors, a worthy pendant to the two composer-performers, Sgambati and Bazzini. As it is, Mancinelli must stand alone as the type of this branch of his art. To Englishmen, at any rate to those who frequent the Royal Opera at Covent Garden, he is a very familiar figure indeed. Since 1888 he has presided at the production of almost every important novelty (except when performed in German) at that hive of industry, besides conducting an endless list of older and more familiar works. A successful *chef d'orchestre* has no time to be an admirable Crichton. In the midst of his multifarious duties Mancinelli has little leisure for composition, and indeed his wonderful gifts as a conductor have gradually elbowed his other talents from the field. He was born in the historic city of Orvieto in 1848 and seems to have picked up his music anyhow. He had very little regular instruction in composition, but learnt the violoncello from Stolci, a talented Florentine performer. It was as a 'cellist that he first faced the world. At the Pergola Theatre in Florence, and afterwards at the Apollo Theatre in Rome, he filled the post of first violoncello. While he was in Rome, his great opportunity came. The conductor suddenly fell ill, and the manager, in despair, was just going to postpone the performance at the last moment, when some good angel whispered in his ear that the first violoncello was an accomplished musician and had the score of " Aida "— for that was the work in question—at his fingers' ends. He called him from the ranks and put him at once at the head of affairs. Everything went off capitally, and Mancinelli's fortune was made. After one or two preliminary trials he had an offer of a post at Bologna. The triple office of Principal of the Liceo

Musicale, Conductor of the Teatro Comunale, and Maestro di Capella of the Church of San Petronio was vacant. Arduous as the duties were, Mancinelli eagerly embraced them. He soon worked wonders in the old university town. He set to work, like Lord Beaconsfield, to educate his followers. He established a symphony and quartet society. He organised concerts, at which the elect of musical Italy conducted or performed their own compositions. He infused new blood into the *répertoire* of the theatre, and, to crown all, wrote an opera himself, "Isora di Provenza," and produced it with gratifying success. Under his *régime*, Bologna, the "Bayreuth of Italy" as somebody christened it, became the centre of Italian musical culture. Beside it Rome was old-fashioned and Milan provincial. But even Bologna was too narrow for so ardent a spirit. After five years within its walls (1881-86) he visited London, and gave a concert at Prince's Hall, in the height of the season. The concert was very successful, and the attention of musical London was directed upon the talented young Italian conductor. I say conductor advisedly, for Mancinelli's own compositions, several of which were included in the programme, did not make so deep an impression as the very remarkable manner in which he interpreted Beethoven's C minor Symphony. Many people were surprised that an Italian should know anything about Beethoven at all. Consequently, when Mancinelli conducted the symphony from memory, and gave a reading of it which for novelty and incisiveness was comparable with that of the most famous German conductors, the critics who had come to scoff remained to applaud.

Mancinelli's success was by no means barren of result. The happy audacity of his attempt to take London by storm deserved some recompense, and a recompense it undoubtedly received, but not perhaps in precisely the shape which the young composer had anticipated. He was requested by the Committee of the Norwich

Triennial Festival to compose an oratorio for
the Festival in the following autumn, and was
secured at the same time by Sir Augustus
Harris as principal conductor for the operatic
compaign which he intended to enter upon at
Drury Lane in 1887.

Mancinelli's remarkable success in the latter
capacity was fully recognised. The season was
a great artistic, if not pecuniary success, and
did much to prove that there was still a public
in London for Italian opera adequately performed and intelligently staged. Mancinelli's
share in this success was not a small one. He,
like his *impresario*, was a sworn foe to the
"star" system, and the care which he devoted to training his band and chorus secured
performances of such all-round excellence as
had not been seen upon the English stage since
the days of Costa.

" Isaias," written to a Latin poem by Giuseppe
Albini, but sung at Norwich to an English
translation, is founded upon a Hebrew legend
connected with the Assyrian siege of Jerusalem

in the reign of Hezekiah. Tradition has it
that, by way of forlorn hope, the maidens of
the city went out to the enemy's camp to
intercede for mercy. They were eagerly welcomed and offered wine. A miracle changed it
into water, and the whole host of Assyrians
were stricken down in the sleep of death, while
the maidens returned uninjured and triumphant
to the liberated city.

Mancinelli's music has many weaknesses,
and at its best proves only that the composer
should never have dreamt of writing an oratorio.
The choral portions of " Isaias " are undeni-
ably feeble. Mancinelli, as indeed is only
natural, is as innocent of the science of counterpoint as a babe unborn. His attempts at
imitative writing would be laughable, if they
were not dull. But there is a good deal of suave
melody in " Isaias," and occasional glimpses
of dramatic power. A stronger man than
Mancinelli was needed for Isaiah's portentous
solo, a monologue, fifteen pages long, in the
vocal score. The orchestration is really the

most successful part of " Isaias;" it is thoroughly operatic in style, brilliant, highly-coloured, and sensuous. But oratorio cannot live by orchestration alone, and " Isaias " has been dismissed to the limbo of unsuccessful Festival novelties.

Since the days of " Isaias," Mancinelli has only once appeared before a London audience in the capacity of composer. This was when the Philharmonic Society performed his Orchestral Suite, "Scene Veneziane," a brilliant trifle, full of dash and go, but not remarkable for the " high seriousness " which Matthew Arnold demanded as the final test of what is really great in art. But it is probably as much from choice as from necessity that Mancinelli has become less and less of a composer and more and more of a conductor. In the latter capacity, so far as it relates to the stage, he has few rivals, and a record of what he has achieved at Covent Garden during the last seven years would be the best proof of his sterling merit.

To one who remembers the old days of scratch companies and "star" artists, the change to the completeness and order of the present *régime* is very remarkable. Mancinelli has done a vast amount of good work at Covent Garden, but perhaps we associate him more particularly with the extremely fine performances of "Lohengrin" which have been given during his dictatorship, with the splendid revival of "Die Meistersinger," and with the performances of Verdi's later works, "Aida," "Otello," and "Falstaff." In these, and indeed in everything he has undertaken, Mancinelli has shown qualities which entitle him to a high place among contemporary operatic conductors.

We are not likely to have many opportunities of renewing acquaintance with him as a composer, for when not at his post in Covent Garden, he is equally hard at work at Madrid or in America, and his moments of leisure for composition must necessarily be few and far between. But in his instance, at any rate, we may feel sure that the general verdict is

not far wrong; and if Mancinelli's busy career
has deprived Italy of a graceful and distinguished
composer, the world at large is the richer for a
conductor, who, on his own ground, is without
a rival

Printed by BALLANTYNE, HANSON & Co.
London & Edinburgh.

www.ingramcontent.com/pod-product-compliance
Lightning Source LLC
Chambersburg PA
CBHW031410270326
41929CB00010BA/1393